MAKE PINTEREST WORK FOR YOUR BUSINESS

The complete guide
to marketing your business,
generating leads, finding
new customers and building
your brand on Pinterest

Alex Stearn

Copyright © 2015 Alex Stearn

All rights reserved

© 2014 by Alex Stearn
AMS Media and Publishing Ltd
Exterior cover, internal design and contents
© Alex Stearn All rights reserved.
The rights to reproduce the work are reserved to the copyright holder.

No part of this publication may be reproduced, stored in a retrieval system, distributed, or transmitted in any form or by any means, electronic or mechanical, photocopying, recording, scanning or otherwise without the prior written permission of the publisher, except in the case of brief quotations embodied in critical reviews and certain other non commercial uses permitted by copyright law. For permission requests, write to the publisher, Alex Stearn. All the business names, product names and brand names used in this book are trademarks, trade names or registered trademarks of their respective owners and I am not associated with any product, business entity or company. The views, opinions and strategies in this book are purely those of the author.

Limit of Liability / Disclaimer of Warranty. While the publisher and author have used their best efforts in preparing this book, they make no representations or warranties with the respect to the accuracy or completeness of the contents of this book specifically disclaim any implied warranties of merchantability or fitness for a particular purpose. No warranty maybe created or extended by sales representatives or written sales materials. The advice and strategies contained herein may not be suitable for your situation. You should consult with a professional where appropriate. Neither the publisher or the author shall be liable for any loss of profit or any commercial damages, including but not limited to special, incidental, consequential, or other damages.

Although the author and publisher have made every effort to ensure that the information in this book was correct at press time, the author and publisher do not assume and hereby disclaim any liability to any party for any loss, damage, or disruption caused by errors or omissions, whether such errors or omissions result from negligence, accident, or any other cause. While every effort is made to ensure that all the information in this book is accurate and up to date, we accept no responsibility for keeping the information up to date or any liability for any failure to do so.

Copyright © 2015 Alex Stearn

Available from Amazon.com CreateSpace eStore and Bookstores and Online Retailers.

AMS Media and Publishing Ltd All rights reserved

This book is dedicated
to Sonia, Tony and Ollie.

Any Questions?

Thank you for your recent purchase of 'Make Pinterest Work for your Business' I really hope you will enjoy the book and your business will benefit greatly.

If you have any questions about the book or about social media marketing in general, please do not hesitate to contact me by email at alex@alexstearn.com or on **Facebook at** www.facebook.com/alexandrastearn and I will do my best to reply as soon as possible. I also offer regular updates, ebooks and social media tips in my newsletter at www.alexstearn.com and a group on Facebook which is all about supporting each other in our social media efforts and networking. Would love you to join us at this link
http://bit.ly/yourgroup

Looking forward to connecting ツ

Why This Book?

SO YOU WANT to launch a Pinterest marketing campaign for your business or maybe you've already done so and you're just not achieving the results you expected. Perhaps that's because you've found it difficult to build a sizeable following or your audience is simply not converting into paying customers.

Every day hundreds of businesses are setting out on their social media journey excited about the opportunities and possibilities that this relatively new type of marketing may be able to offer their business. Some are getting it right, reaping huge rewards, and managing to leverage the enormous power of the Internet through social media, but the majority are struggling to make it work at all. Those who are struggling often don't really understand exactly how social media works and launch into a campaign without any plan or strategy or without even knowing exactly what they are looking to achieve. They perhaps create a Pinterest page and ask their web developer to add a 'like' or 'follow' button to their website, invite their friends and customers to join their page, and then start posting updates. After a while they realize that whatever they are doing is having little or no positive effect on their sales and they are left with the same questions:

- How do I leverage the almighty power of the Internet and Pinterest to make money for my business?
- How do I find the people who are interested in my products?
- How do I draw these people away from Pinterest and onto my website or blog?
- And the ultimate question, how do I convert all these people into

paying customers and actually profit from Pinterest marketing?

These businesses either continue to go round in circles waiting for a miracle to happen, give up altogether, or continue to believe that there is a way they can make social media work for their business and start looking for a solution to solve their problem.

This is exactly what I did and this is where my social media journey began. I started to look for a solution but kept coming up with the same brick walls, the same fluffy vague information about engagement, and lots of very expensive courses. I read books and blogs but they never really seemed to solve my problem and get to the heart of the matter.

I then decided to make it my mission to demystify the hype surrounding social media marketing and discover everything I possibly could about how to make all the major social media platforms work for any business. I studied literally hundreds of campaigns to see what was working and what wasn't and completely immersed myself in social media marketing until all my questions were answered. My aim was to discover how to utilize the almighty power of Pinterest to help any business achieve their marketing goals. I made it my mission to leave no stone unturned in terms of a marketing opportunity which could help any business generate leads and ultimately increase their sales.

After 18 months of immersing myself in this subject, I am now delighted to hand this information over to you. My goal is to help you save your time and your resources and provide you with a highly effective system to make Pinterest work for your business. In this book I am going to share with you everything you need to know to take your business to the next level and leverage the power of Pinterest so you can achieve the highest profits, the best customers, the best ambassadors for your business, and make money 24/7.

This book is perfect for anyone who is seriously committed to growing their business and achieving incredible results. Whether you are just starting out or already up and running and uncertain how to make Pinterest work for your business then this book is to going to teach you exactly how to do just that. You will have absolutely everything you need to learn, prepare, plan, and implement a campaign which is going to help you generate leads and find new customers.

The fact is, Pinterest, and social media as a whole, is a game changer, a dream come true for any business and has completely revolutionized the way business is being done today. However, it is still just a marketing tool and while on the face of it seems free, if not used correctly and effectively, it is simply just a waste of your time and resources.

In this book you will not only learn the skills and strategies of Pinterest marketing but also everything you need to know about how social media works in marketing and how to plan, prepare, and execute your campaign including:

- What social media marketing is, why it is so good, why it is absolutely essential for any business today, and why so many businesses are getting it wrong
- The psychology behind why people make buying decisions and how you can use this knowledge to succeed in your Pinterest campaign and other social media campaigns as well
- The importance of defining your business, your brand, and your target audience and how to do this
- How to set clear goals and objectives for your social media campaign
- How to prepare your website or blog for success, capture leads, and build a highly targeted list of subscribers
- How to plan, create, maintain, and manage your Pinterest campaign
- Detailed information about how to set up your business profile

- on Pinterest
- The strategies you need to implement to attract the best prospects and build and maintain a targeted following on Pinterest and build lasting relationships
- The importance of content and how to easily find ideas to create content for your page
- How to convert your followers into leads, paying customers, and ambassadors and brand advocates of your business
- How to constantly measure and monitor your campaign so you can steer your campaign to achieve your goals

A great deal of love and joy has gone into writing this book. Love of the subject itself and joy at the opportunity to share with you the information and knowledge within. I have devoted 18 months to researching and writing this book, along with the others in the series, in order to uncover the truth about social media. I truly hope you will be inspired and that your business will thrive and flourish by implementing the suggested strategies.

As mentioned above there are books available on Kindle and in paperback for each of the major social media platforms including Twitter and Periscope, LinkedIn, Google + YouTube, Instagram, Pinterest and Tumblr. The big book, 'Make Social Media Work for your Business' covers the whole series. As the sections on social media marketing are common to all books then I would suggest that if you are planning to purchase others in the series, it would be better value for you to purchase this book rather than each individual book. The big book 'Make Social Media Work for your Business' is available from $9.99 at this Link

Even within the time it has taken to write this book, certain things have changed in the social media world and so some sections have been updated to reflect those changes. The world of social media is dynamic and therefore it is my commitment to keep updating this book as and when those changes occur. If you wish to keep up-to-date with latest social media updates, tips, and changes, please subscribe to my newsletter at www.alexstearn.com

Chapter One

The Importance of Understanding Social Media Marketing

BEFORE LAUNCHING INTO your Pinterest marketing campaign, and so that you are absolutely committed when you do start, you will need to be convinced that social media marketing does actually work for businesses and that you are going to be able to make it work for yours. In this chapter, you will learn why social media marketing has gained so much attention, why so many brands are using it, and why it is so different from other forms of marketing. The aim here is to help you truly appreciate the power and importance of this relatively new method of marketing. Once you are totally convinced that the time you will be investing will be truly worthwhile, you will be ready to launch into your Pinterest marketing campaign with strength, confidence, and conviction.

So what is social media exactly? Social media is the place where people connect with other people using the technology we have today. It's where people engage, share, cooperate, interact, learn, enjoy, and build relationships. The number of ways in which we connect with each other has grown massively in recent years from telephone, mobiles, email, text, video, newspaper, or radio to what we have today, the social media networks.

As humans, the majority of us want to belong, be accepted, loved, respected, and heard. We are social animals and social media has provided us with new tools which allow us to be more social, even if our lives are more hectic and we are living a long way from our friends and family. It's now not unusual for family and friends to be located at opposite sides of the country or even in a different country. Our lives have become far busier and more transient than ever, and yet we still crave the same social connections as we did 100 years ago when we would probably have been living in the same village or town as our family and friends.

The impact that social media is having on our lives and on businesses is massive. Social media has completely changed the way we communicate and the way we do everything. It has made connecting with people and building relationships so much easier. Now, staying in contact with someone we may only have met once is straightforward. We can find old friends we went to school or college with, and the opportunities for making new contacts are limitless. Social media has given us the ability to quickly and easily share ideas, experiences, and information on anything we like, and we can find out about anyone, any business, or anything. With the massive growth in smartphone ownership, most people can now access the internet instantly. We are living in a virtual world and we can literally connect to anyone, from anywhere, at anytime.

Understanding the reasons why people love social media so much will help give you a really good idea about how, as a business, you need to engage so you can connect with your audience and grow and maintain that audience. Most people are on social media to be social, to connect with other family and friends, and to have fun. However, here are a few more reasons why so many use and love social media:

To be part of a community or common interest group
To express their feelings and have a voice
To reconnect with old college or school friends
To find out where their friends are
To tell their friends where they are
To announce a piece of news
To find out if a product or service is good

To connect with thought leaders
To make business contacts
To follow brands
To keep up-to-date with current affairs, football scores
To connect with famous people
To find inspiration and motivation
To learn by reading blogs, watching videos, and listening to podcasts
To help other people
To launch a business
To advertise and grow a business
To make new friends
To make new contacts
To connect with others in different countries
To make a difference
To be entertained
To communicate quickly and save time
To support important causes or people
To find a job

The power and enormity of social media

Everyone is doing Social! Okay, so not everyone is doing social media, but the majority of people are! Wherever you go you will see somebody with their heads down looking at some device, and you can bet your bottom dollar that they are accessing some social site, whether it's Pinterest , Twitter, Instagram, LinkedIn, YouTube, Google+, Pinterest, or Snapchat.

The growth in social media is huge, and it's no wonder that it is being called 'The Social Media Revolution.' Without going into too much statistical information, it's safe to say that your customer is probably using at least one social network, either for personal or business use, and very likely to be accessing multiple sites.

All the social media platforms are growing at incredible speeds. You only have to type 'Social media statistics' into Google and you will blown away by the millions and billions. Facebook now has over one billion users and 95% of those users access it at least once a day and some more than five times. More than one billion unique users visit YouTube per month, and Twitter has 215 monthly active users. The most popular websites are social. The world loves social.

WHAT IS SOCIAL MEDIA MARKETING

Not long ago promoting a business could feel very much like being alone on a desert island. You could have a great idea but unless you had vast sums of money for television, magazine, or direct mail advertising then, frustratingly, your idea was very likely to remain a secret. Today it is totally different and social media has given businesses endless opportunities to reach their target audience, connect with new prospects, and enter new markets. The playing field has been leveled out, and now anyone with the right knowledge has more chance than ever of making their business a success.

Social media marketing is a relatively new form of marketing and refers to the processes, strategies, and tactics used by businesses on social networking sites and blogs to gain attention and ultimately increase their revenue. Businesses and large brands are now using the fact that people love to engage and connect with other people with the other very important fact that they are very likely to find their target audience on social media so that they can do the following:

- Find, reach, and connect with potential customers
- Drive traffic to a website or blog
- Stay connected and communicate with existing customers. It is a well-known fact that existing customers are far more likely to purchase and also pay more for a product than someone who has not bought before.
- To build trust, interest, and loyalty by interacting with your followers (potential customers) so that ultimately they will

purchase your product, continue to purchase your product, and hopefully recommend your product to their friends
- To produce content that users will share with their social network or recommend to their friends. Social media marketing strongly centers around the creation of content for a particular audience with the intention that it can be shared, 'liked', and commented on by the user. When this happens, the content is being passed to other users by word-of-mouth, the most powerful form of advertising.
- To listen and find out what your customers want

THE BIG LINK, THE PSYCHOLOGY BEHIND BUYING BEHAVIOUR

Not only have successful marketeers recognized that people want to engage with people, they have also tapped into the psychology behind why people make buying decisions and incorporated this into their social media campaigns.

As a business you will need to understand a great deal about your customers in order to market your products successfully to your target audience. Understanding how and why people make the final purchase decision will go a long way to help you discern how to make social media marketing actually work for your business. There seem to be a number of common factors that influence consumers when they are making their buying decision. Leveraging and using this knowledge with your Facebook campaign will be incredibly powerful and a recipe for success.

The 'like' factor

This is a biggie. When we look at the findings and the psychology behind buying decisions it often comes down to simply being likeable. Consumers are far more likely to buy a product from someone they like, respect, or trust. Word-of-mouth advertising has always proven to be the most powerful form of advertising and now Facebook has taken this to another level and managed to harness this online with the 'like' button. Having your business name or brand reach hundreds or even thousands of people is now possible, and someone only has to 'like' or interact with your business on social media and you can almost guarantee that someone else will see that interaction. The truth is people do business with people they like and are more likely to spread the word to their network about deals and special offers from people they like, trust, and respect.

Social proof

When a consumer finds themselves at a point of indecision they will look for social proof and seek advice and corroboration from others. They are far more likely to buy if they see that their friends or a similar group of people have bought or used product. People generally look to others for advice or look to see what others are buying to get over their personal insecurity when making a buying decision. This is why you see so many women shopping in pairs. The opinion of a friend about an item can often be the deciding factor when making the decision to buy or not.

Facebook is one of the most trusted platforms when it comes to product or service recommendations. This is where the Facebook plug-ins come in. They actually display social proof by showing the faces of your friends or a number count of the people who 'liked' the product, article, or page. The reason this is so powerful with social media marketing is simply because seeing a large number of people 'liking' a product or service can be enough to persuade someone to make a buying decision, to read something, or to follow a business. The truth is that people trust the opinion of others more than they trust advertising, and in order to make social media marketing work then businesses need to leverage this fact.

Authority and reviews

Even before the Internet was introduced, people were keen to find reviews about products they were interested in buying, particularly if they were planning to make a major purchase. They would either buy a special magazine or seek information from an authoritative figure on a TV advertisement. Today, however, shoppers are far more savvy. They can smell an advert a mile off and they will go out of their way to find honest reviews about something they may want to buy. They are also spoilt for choice, not only with the number of products available to them but the fact that they can find a review about literally anything just by a simple search on the Internet or looking at a brand's social media profile. People always have and always will want as much evidence as possible that they are making the right buying decision. Any business who wants to succeed today needs to embrace this fact and try and gain as many reviews for their products and services as possible. Reviews could be in the form of customer blog articles, reviews on your website, on social media sites, or articles in newspapers and magazines. Displaying articles, client testimonials, or the logos of magazines that you have been featured in on your website will also go a long way to building authority and gaining the trust of your prospects.

Scarcity or exclusivity

Scarcity or exclusivity can play a big part in people's buying decisions, and Pinterest is a perfect place to communicate and use this factor to sell your products. If a product is scarce or less available, the consumer will often perceive that this product has greater value. As they become less available, the consumer fears that they may lose out on a great deal or a one-time offer. Giving your prospects a deadline or a specific time to purchase something or redeem an offer is an incredibly powerful way of focusing their mind to make a decision. When they know they need to make that decision by a certain time or they may lose out on a one-time deal, they are far more likely to make that decision. Another very effective way of using this factor is by simply suggesting to your prospects that by signing up for your email opt-in, they will be the first to hear about your new products or your exclusive offers.

Loyalty

Consumers do not like taking risks and often prefer to repeat their past purchasing behavior by buying from a brand they have bought from before. The majority of shoppers are brand loyal and social media is another way of nurturing this type of behavior by building up even deeper relationships with your customers through constant contact and updates.

Reciprocation

Reciprocation is a very powerful factor to take into consideration if you are looking to succeed on Pinterest . As humans, the majority of us have a natural desire to repay favors and with Pinterest you can really put this into practice. If you show support by either 'liking', sharing, or commenting on other people's content, not only will it attract their attention, they will, more often than not, return the favor by 'liking', commenting, and sharing your content. Also, if you are sharing great content on your network or offering good, valuable, and free advice, you are very likely to earn a great deal of respect. This will often result in a good payback of some sort later.

Why is Social Media Marketing So Good for your Business?

We know that an enormous number of people are accessing the social networks to connect with each other, and now we need to understand why this type of marketing is so different from other forms of marketing and why it is so important for your business. The main reason is that social media marketing is fundamentally more effective. Consumers today are smart. They are tired and suspicious of traditional forms of advertising. More often than not they will fast forward a TV commercial, switch channels, or skip a printed page with an advertisement on it. Today's consumers want to hear that a product has been tried and tested. They want to see a product being demonstrated, and they often need a recommendation from a trusted source, most likely a fried, to make a purchase. Here are some reasons why social media marketing is more effective than other, more traditional, marketing methods:

Social media offers you the opportunity to find the right target audience.
Never before has it been so easy to find and access your target audience. With the information that Pinterest and most of the social networks hold about their users, you can now target and find the very people who are more likely to buy your products or services.

Social media allows you to have direct contact with your customer.
You literally have the opportunity to communicate directly and stay in touch with your customer, unlike traditional forms of advertising.

Social media marketing harnesses the power of peer recommendation.
The majority of people trust recommendations by others. Social media marketing is the only media that can harness the most powerful form of advertising, word of mouth, by making it possible for consumers to communicate with each other and vote for products or services by pressing the 'like' or 'follow' button.

Social media helps builds your brand.
Never has there been so much opportunity to build your brand. Your brand is simply the most valuable asset of your business. Your brand is what differentiates you from other businesses. It is the image people have of your business, and it establishes loyalty. With social media you have the opportunity to engage with consumers and build positive brand associations in a way that no other media can. Consumers now have the choice and opportunity to follow your brand. If they do, this means they actually want to hear or see what you have to say.

Social media humanizes your brand.
Social media allows you to communicate with your audience in a totally unique way. Your brand is no longer a rigid logo but a personality. Not only can you show your appreciation and the value you place on your

audience, but they can also grow to love your brand too. No other type of marketing allows this type of two-way live communication.

Offers continual exposure to your product.
Social media marketing allows you to be continually in contact with your followers. Once you build your audience, they can hear from you and see your brand on a daily basis. Statistics prove that, on average, a person needs to see or connect with a brand seven times before purchasing. This is a difficult and costly goal to achieve with traditional forms of advertising but incredibly easy with social media marketing.

The consumer has a choice.
Unlike other traditional methods of advertising, the consumer has the opportunity to be exposed to your product by choice. They can opt in or out whenever they want.

Your audience is relaxed and receptive.
The majority of people are accessing Pinterest and other social media accounts in their own leisure time to be social. Social media is all about connecting with friends and relatives, meeting new people and making new contacts. People are far more receptive to hearing from a brand in their own time when they are relaxed, as long as the brand is offering some kind of value and is not continually pushing their product.

You can continually engage with your audience.
Social media marketing allows businesses to have an ongoing dialogue with their audience like no other media. Fans or followers who have interacted with a business on social media are far more likely to visit their online store than those who did not.

It's viral.
Once your followers choose to interact or share your content then this interaction is seen by their network of friends who are then also exposed to your brand. This is how viral growth happens, which results in

audience growth and brand awareness, more prospects, more customers, and increased sales.

Social media is an asset to your business.
Unlike other forms of advertising where you see your marketing investment disappear, your Pinterest account, or any other social media account, becomes a valuable asset. If you are using your social media marketing correctly, your network will grow, you will be building trust, and your asset will increase in value. With traditional advertising, once an advert is delivered the connection with the buyer is over and you see your investment literally disappear.

It is like having your own broadcasting channel.
Once you have your campaign set up and your follower numbers are growing, you literally have your very own broadcasting channel which you own. You can communicate with your followers about anything 24/7. Nobody can take this away unless, of course, you are not running it correctly and you are losing followers. If you provide content that is so useful and interesting, your followers will keep coming back again and again to check if you have anything new to say. You then have a following of people who will associate your valuable content and their positive experience with your brand.

You can offer your customers proof of trading.
Having a social media presence that is active and engaging helps reassure customers that your business actually exists. They can easily check, by comments left by customers, whether your business is reputable and trustworthy. They are far more likely to buy from you once they see your active presence on social media.

Social media improves your search engine ranking.
Google counts social sharing when ranking your website or blog. If people are finding your content valuable then the search engines will register this and rank your site accordingly. Social media sites are highly

ranked in the search engines and having a well-optimized profile is yet another way of being found on the Internet.

Social media opens up a worldwide playing field.
It used to be only the large companies who could afford to build their brand and have the opportunity to access thousands of potential customers. Now everybody with a business has the opportunity to reach thousands of people, both nationally and globally, grow their business, and benefit from one of the most powerful forms of marketing. Having a business no longer needs be a lonely island. You literally have the opportunity to get your message heard by thousands of people through social networking.

Social media provides advantages for the consumer.
With just a few clicks of the mouse or the tap of a smartphone, consumers can be in contact with any business very quickly. For the first time they have a very powerful voice. Their opinions are taken seriously. They are and valued whether they are in contact through customer service or just following a brand because they are interested. People want to remain close to the brands they are interested in, and this is shown by the continual rise in the number of people following brands.

You can listen to your customers.
You can now hear what your customers are saying about your product or service, and you can use this information to improve or develop your products and customer service. This helps your business become more transparent and shows your customers that you care and value their opinion, which ultimately leads to more trust for your brand.

You can become a thought leader.
By producing valuable and rich content for your audience, you can become a thought leader. Not only will this help if you are a personal brand, but it will also help build trust and reputation for any business or brand.

You can make a difference.
With social media you can actually make a positive difference in people's lives. Once you know your audience, you can provide content which is of value to them and will actually help them in some way. Helping your audience like this goes a long way in helping them remember your business when they are ready to make that purchasing decision.

It promotes endless opportunities.
Never has there been so much opportunity to have direct access to so many people, and neither has there been so much opportunity for any business of any size to have ongoing contact with so many of their potential customers. This is a marketeer or business owner's dream.

Is Social Media Actually Working for Business?

It is evident that the majority of major brands are running successful social media marketing campaigns. These brands are investing huge amounts of money, time, and resources into this type of marketing. However, you don't have to go too far to see whether social media marketing is actually working for business. Simply ask yourself these questions:

• Would you prefer to buy a product if you knew that a friend or somebody you know had tried it?
• Would you prefer to buy a product from a business or person that you do know rather than a one you don't know?
• If you were thinking of buying a product from a business you had no history with, would you go and look to see if they had a social media site and find out what other people were saying about their product?

If you answered yes to these questions then you can be pretty sure that social media marketing does actually work for businesses. It has to, doesn't it?

Why So Many Businesses are Getting it Wrong

Even though most business owners have heard how powerful social media marketing can be, the majority are still unsure as to how to use it to benefit their business. So many social media business accounts have been created with enthusiasm only to be abandoned a couple of months, even weeks, down the line. Others are painstakingly posting consistently every day but posting the wrong type of content without a clue how to get their fans to buy their products. Many businesses are just paying lip service and seem to think that displaying a few social media icons on their site is enough to miraculously increase their revenue, and some are not even connected to any networks at all. Although on the face of it social media marketing seems free, it actually takes a sizeable investment of man hours, and if you are getting it wrong, you may as well be throwing a great deal of money out of the window. Here are some common reasons why so many businesses are getting it wrong:

Not 100% committed and convinced
Many businesses are not convinced that it actually works at all and therefore are not prepared to put in the time it takes to learn how to plan and implement the effective strategies it takes to build a successful campaign. As a result, their campaign falls flat and they simply give up after a few months.

Little or no understanding about how social media marketing works
Many still think that setting up a profile and putting an icon on their website is what it's all about. They may even post a few status updates and post some pictures of their product in the hope that their website is suddenly going to be inundated with new traffic and think that these new visitors are miraculously going to convert into customers.

They don't understand the fact that fans and followers are worthless unless they know what to do with them
Just because a business has maybe 1000 or 30,000 fans or followers, it

does not mean this will automatically transfer to their balance sheet. Fans are just fans, and as long a business doesn't know what do with those fans, they will stay as fans and not customers.

Not understanding the psychology behind buying decisions
They have absolutely no idea about the psychology behind how and why people make buying decisions and, therefore, do not know how to use this knowledge to their advantage in their campaign.

Lack of clear goals
Aimlessly sharing content on their network without setting specific and measurable goals is just a waste of time and resources.

Not having a system to capture and convert leads
Building a following is almost useless if those followers are not visiting the business' website or subscribing to the newsletter so that they can be converted into paying customers. Many businesses are still not making lead capture one of their main goals.

Unrealistic expectations
Social media is a long-term strategy. It needs to be an integral part of a business' marketing plan, and today, it's as important as any other daily task a business may undertake. It is not a one-size-fits-all solution and is not a solution for overnight success. It takes careful planning and long-term commitment.

The wrong audience
It's no good having a huge number of fans if they are not interested in buying your product. There are even sites where you can buy fans, but if they are not the right audience, they are very unlikely to be interested in what that business has to offer.

Not enough followers
The majority of businesses are going to need a sizeable audience to make

any impact at all. Although engagement is important, unless a business has a healthy number of followers, it's not going to be a great deal of benefit.

Not being proactive

Many businesses seem to assume that people are just going to press the 'like' or 'follow' button on their blog or website. Unfortunately it doesn't work like that and people generally need a good reason or incentive to follow a business, unless it's a very well-known brand.

Trying to push their products all the time

This is not what social media marketing is about. Businesses that continually push their products are just missing the whole point of how social media marketing works and will lose followers as a result.

Posting too little, posting too often, or posting the wrong content altogether

If you post too much, your posts will be considered spam. If you post too little, you will just be forgotten. If you post the wrong content, you will not attract the right audience which may harm your brand. The top three reasons for losing fans are:

i.) The company posts too frequently
ii.) The business pushes their products too much
iii.) The business posts offensive content

Chapter Two

How to Run a Successful Pinterest Marketing Campaign, an Overview

ONCE YOU HAVE made the decision to be 100% committed to your campaign, you fully understand the theory behind it, and you plan and implement the strategies and tactics outlined in this book your business is going to reap the benefits and you will in time develop an extremely valuable asset. One thing is for certain: if you choose to ignore social media, you can be sure that your competition will not and you'll be allowing them to steal the advantage. Social media is a powerful way to increase your revenue by driving sales, increasing customer loyalty, and building your brand while at the same time pushing down your cost of sales, marketing, customer service, and much more. Now let's get started!

So how do you leverage the power of social media and put it to work to benefit your business and produce amazing results? This chapter is designed to give you a brief overview about what is required to build a successful campaign so that as and when you read each chapter it will make more sense. Every aspect of this overview and everything you need to do and implement will be mapped out in more detail in the subsequent chapters.

The opportunity to reach an unlimited number of new contacts and prospects is available to every business today. You can safely say that your prospects are out there and all you need to do is know where to find them, how to connect with them, and how to capture and convert them into your customers.

Successful businesses are using Pinterest and the other social media platforms in a totally different way from traditional methods of marketing. WithPinterest marketing there is no need to employ pushy sales techniques. Once you put the essential work, planning, and system in place, you will find your products are practically selling themselves and your prospects are buying your products and becoming your brand advocates as a natural progression from your initial contact with them. The whole process is straight forward and as long as you carry out the necessary background work, planning, and preparation, you can make it work for your business.

Know what you want

You need to have a very good idea where you want your business to be in the next one to three years. If you don't know what you want, then it is unlikely that your business will achieve anywhere near its potential. When you have a clear vision for your business, it helps you to focus and create the necessary goals you need to put into place to achieve that vision.

Define your business, brand, and target audience

Brands establish customer loyalty, and Pinterest offers you a huge opportunity to build your brand. In order to communicate in the right way, you need to create and consistently deliver the right message and brand experience to your prospects and customers. To do this, you need to define your business and define and understand your target audience so you can create your brand.

Plan, plan, plan

Social media is not a quick fix. The majority of businesses start a campaign and then fall by the wayside. If you want to grow your business, then careful planning is required and it will involve creating your mission statement, setting clear and measurable goals and objectives, and planning your content strategy in line with who and what your target audience wants. Without a carefully crafted plan your campaign is extremely unlikely to reach its full potential.

Prepare your business

Before launching your campaign you need to prepare your whole business so your brand and your brand message are evident throughout. You will need to communicate your brand through everything your do or say, including all your marketing material, brochures, promotional material, your website, your blog, and your email.

Your website is one of the best sales people you can have. It works 24/7 and can help to make your business turn up in your customer's home at the click of a mouse. When your prospect arrives on your website it immediately needs to make them feel that they have arrived at the right place, that you understand their needs, and that you can either provide a solution or give them exactly what they want. If you already have a website, you need to check that it has all the necessary features it takes to grab your visitors' attention, deliver the right message, capture them, and convert them into customers. Statistics prove that unless a business has a clever method of capturing leads, the majority of visitors to a website will leave without buying anything or ever returning again. Therefore, before even starting your Pinterest campaign, you will need to check or create your website so that it does the job it is supposed to, which is to capture leads for later sales conversion.

Set up your email campaign

Email is still one of the most effective methods of converting leads, and an up-to-date list of prospects who have given their permission for you to contact them on a regular basis has got to be one of your business' most valuable assets. Capturing email addresses on your website and through social media needs to be your most important marketing goal. Therefore, you will need to plan your opt-in campaign and set up an account with an email provider so you can continue to build a relationship with your prospects and sell your products.

6. Create your Pinterest profile

Your Pinterest profile, your pins and your boards will in many cases be the first impression your prospects have about your business and is as important as your website or blog. The aim of your Pinterest profile is to capture your prospects so that you can continue to communicate and build a relationship with them through their newsfeed and through email. It is unlikely that the majority of your followers will return to your profile after their initial visit so your profile needs to grab their attention and make your prospects take action as soon as they arrive by either following your profile or one of your boards.

Create your Pinterest posting calendar

Social media is not like traditional forms of advertising, so frequently pushing your products, posting adverts, and plugging your business is not going to work and is likely to lose you fans. One of the most important things you are going to have to do for a successful Pinterest campaign is to regularly produce and post compelling content that your audience actually wants to engage with and share. Pinterest marketing is all about selling without selling, and the aim of producing content is not to directly sell your products but to do the following:

- Boost traffic to your blog or website, generate, capture, and nurture leads
- Create brand awareness
- Constantly remind your audience of your brand so when they are ready to buy, they buy from you
- Improve your ranking in the search engines
- Create engagement, build relationships, and encourage your audience to share your content with their friends
- Support others by 'liking', commenting on, and sharing their content
- Stand out as a thought leader and build your reputation as an expert in your industry

- Create such good content that your audience stays 'liking' your page and continuing to read your updates, which builds and encourages brand loyalty.

Your content is where you can connect with your audience through their interests and passions. Your quality of content needs to be outstanding and you need to delight your audience with the best possible fresh, new, and compelling material. Excellence is what you should be aiming for with every update you make. The biggest thing to remember is that you need to tailor all your content to your audience's desires and needs.

Once you are absolutely clear about who your target audience is, what makes them tick, and what their values and aspirations are, you can determine what subjects and topics they will be interested in. The majority of the content you post will need to be about their needs and not yours. There is nothing more off putting and likely to lose you followers than continually posting about your business and shouting about your products or services. Of course you can do this occasionally if you have a new product or a special offer, but you need to be selective. Otherwise, your posts just become bad noise. Remember your followers are mostly on social media to be social. If your posts ruin their social experience, they will associate your brand with a bad experience and it won't be long before you start losing your fans and potential customers.

When you have decided on the subjects and topics you are going to create content about, you will need to create a Pinterest posting calendar which will help you to consistently deliver this high-quality content. You will need to incorporate everything in this calendar, including any events you are planning, any special industry events, public holidays, blog posts, videos, and offers or contests you may be planning. You then need to map it all out so you know exactly how you are going to promote them on Pinterest with the functionality you have available to do so.

Build a sizeable and highly targeted following

The main aim of building your audience is to grow a community of followers who are interested in your products, will engage with your content, and become advocates for your brand. In order to have any impact at all you are going to need a sizeable number of targeted fans on Pinterest . Building your audience will be an ongoing task, and it involves many different strategies which will be covered in this book. The size of audience and time it takes will depend on the time and resources you have available.

The essential day-to-day activity
To build a strong presence, trust, relationships, and reputation, you will need to be active and nurture your fans. Social media is not a one-way street. It's an ongoing two-way communication. It's about going out and showing that you are interested in what others have to say, and it's about building community and getting your brand out there in the most positive light possible. Here are some of the things you will need to do on a day-to-day basis:

- Consistently post high-quality content
- Follow your followers and fans
- Engage, comment, share, and reply
- Show your audience you value and respect them
- Follow influencers in your niche
- Deal with negative comments

Analyzing and measuring your campaign results
This book is all about how to make Pinterest work for your business, and the only way you are going to find out if it is working or not is by constantly monitoring and analyzing your results. You will need to constantly check your results against the goals and objectives you have set. Once you know what is working and what is not then you can adjust and steer your campaign accordingly to achieve more positive results.

Chapter Three

Getting Started on Pinterest

PINTEREST HAS TO be the most, exciting, delicious, beautiful and captivating of all the social media platforms. When you initially set up your account, if you haven't already done so, it won't surprise you that this was the fastest site in history to cross the 10 million member mark.

The marketing possibilities and opportunities are endless and a dream come true for businesses of all kinds because the typical person who is using Pinterest not only shops but they also tend to be high spenders too.

Once you discover how this platform is being used by millions for their personal use and truly appreciate why Pinterest has grown and continues to grow at this incredible rate you will see why this platform may be one of the most powerful forces for marketing your business.

What is Pinterest?

Pinterest is a social bookmarking tool and content sharing site used to 'pin' images, videos and other objects found on the internet to a virtual pin board. People join to create, organize and share the collections of the things they love and then share them with their friends if they wish.

When you join Pinterest you can literally take images from the internet with the click of the 'pin it' button and pin them to a board. Pins always link back to the website source. A board is where you organize your collection of pins by topic/subject of your choice.

The site seems to make everything possible for its users by helping them to create the lifestyle they are striving for on a pin board. Their pin board is like a personal statement saying here are some of the beautiful things that I love and make me who I am or and this is how I want my life to be.

Pinterest is great for personal use because you can create boards about anything you like and can collect as much information as you like and then find it all in one place. It's like having your own personal magazine, the main difference being it consists only of the things you love.

The concept seems so simple yet Ben Silberman and his co founders have surpassed excellence and made the Pinterest experience completely unique, beautiful and fascinating for their users. It is no wonder it took four months and 50 working variations of the site before they came up with the final grid design. Another of the main features of the site is the 'Infinite Scroll'. The never ending page lets users browse more and more images without having to click buttons and waist time waiting for pages to load.

The founders were also very discerning about how they built their initial audience realising the beauty of the site would result mainly from the images pinned. What emerged was a growing community of mid western young american women pinning ideas for weddings, home design and recipes. However, the audience has grown into much more.

As a child, Ben Silberman was fascinated with nature and was a great collector of everything from insects to stamps. "What you collect says so much about who you are" he said in an interview.

When you log into your account you are welcomed by your home feed which is made up of images from all those you are following, it's this beauty and simplicity which makes Pinterest so unique and so appealing to its users. It was designed to be visually appealing with a minimum of text. It is the ultimate window shopping experience which makes it a dream come true for businesses. "When you open up Pinterest," Ben Silberman says, "you should feel like you've walked into a building full of stuff that only you are interested in. Everything should feel handpicked for you."

Pinterest is also a social platform and like all the others you can follow, share your content by repinning , make comments and tag users. However the similarities stop there and Pinterest succeeds with the uniqueness of its product and a very different audience. The majority of Pinterest users are actively looking for inspiration and whether they are looking for wedding ideas, home and interior ideas, fashion ideas or recipes they are ready to buy. Pinterest boasts very high sales conversion rates.

Once 'Pinners' have found what they like there is a good chance they will visit the website source, share by repinning on one of their boards and then someone else will see it on their board. This is what makes Pinterest so viral.

Why is Pinterest so Good for Business?

Pinterest has become a social media platform which is hard to ignore for businesses selling directly to consumers and for those selling to other businesses. While starting as a hang out for middle class American women looking for lifestyle inspiration it is now become much more. Every day millions of people are using Pinterest to look for inspiration, buy products and connect with others who have similar interests. The majority of users are still women residing in the US but Pinterest is now growing a much stronger presence in Canada, Australia and the UK. To help your decide whether you think it could be a part of your marketing plan here are some of the main reasons why using Pinterest to market your business maybe very good idea:

Excellent traffic referral

Pinterest is a top generator and referrer of website traffic and statistics report that buyers referred to sites by Pinterest are 10% more likely to buy. Businesses who have installed the 'Pin it' button have seen big increases in traffic.

Easy to find and target your audience
Since the whole Pinterest concept is interest based and you can search by interest, finding your target audience and building up a community of people who are very likely to be interested in your products has been made possible.

A new and interested audience
Pinterest's fast growing audience is very different from other social media networks because users are using the site for inspiration. Unlike Facebook or Twitter their first priority for being on Pinterest is probably not to be social but to actively search out new products. This makes this audience one that is much more ready to purchase. Pinterest offers a delicious visual experience for users and the average time spent on Pinterest is one hour. Moreover statistics are proving that Pinterest is a major player when it comes to people purchasing. According to www.comscore.com Pinterest buyers spend more money, more often, and on more items than any of the other top 5 social media sites.

Higher Spending audience
It has been reported that Pinterest shoppers spend more per session, in comparison with Facebook shoppers.

Levels the playing field
With Pinterest your frustration of getting your products out there can be over. Everything is possible for everyone and you don't have to be a big brand to compete and if you have a new product, a new gadget or invention there seems to be no better place to showcase it. Because of the amazing visual experience that the site layout offers, every business has the opportunity to make their products look appealing. Pinterest is all

about discovery and a great place for your potential customers to discover what you have to offer. Once you find your target audience the chances are that their friends will have a similar taste and suddenly you have a growing community.

Simplicity

The beauty of Pinterest is its simplicity and it has mastered visual sharing. Pinterest has managed to leverage the strength of social proof and word of mouth advertising with the simplicity and visual power of images.

Branding

Because of its visual nature Pinterest offers businesses the perfect platform to build their brand with images that reflect their brand.

Information about customers

No other social media site gives you as much insight into what your customers' interests and desires are, as Pinterest. Pinterest is where their members go to showcase what they are passionate about and then share it with their friends. Simply by visiting your audience's profiles and looking at their pins and boards will give you so much information about their lifestyle and desires. Getting to know them like this will not only help you tailor your marketing efforts but also help you to build on the products that you can offer .

The path from seeing a product to buying it is shorter

Visitors from Pinterest convert into customers much faster than from any other social network. It seems that the step from seeing to buying is more natural and displaying your products doesn't come over as being pushy because the visual display of images is what Pinterest is all about. The saying, 'A picture paints a thousand words' truly comes into play on Pinterest.

Huge Viral Potential

Pins flourish virally and currently 80% of pins are repins which means a huge amount of sharing is going on and shared images are being circulated more than new images are being uploaded. User engagement on Pinterest is very high and this is because of the visual nature of the platform. It seems it is totally addictive and users can't stop sharing.

Your content has a long shelf life
Because Pinterest is interest based rather than timeline based your content will be still relevant and shared long after it has been posted.

Easy to manage & less costly
The great thing about Pinterest is it is simple and because your content stays current for longer, managing this platform is very much easier than the other social networking platforms as you are not under the constant pressure of time.

Website integration
Pinterest is so easy to integrate into your website. By simply placing a button on your site your visual content can be instantly shared with others. Literally one image from your site could be shared and repinned hundreds of times.

Facebook and Twitter integration
Users can now automatically post pins to their Facebook news feed and Twitter accounts.

Search engine optimization
Pinterest is indexed by Google and is another way to get found and a good way of obtaining valuable back links to your site. After all if people are pinning your pins, then this means people like your content and this is what Google are looking for and Google likes websites with authentic back links.

IS PINTEREST RELEVANT FOR YOUR BUSINESS?

Only you will be able to tell whether it will be worth investing your time and resources on this platform and it mostly comes down to whether your customers are on Pinterest or not, and what you are selling. The majority of users are still women residing in the US but Pinterest is now growing a much stronger presence in Canada, Australia and the UK. Here is a list of the top ten categories on Pinterest:

- Home
- Arts and Crafts
- Style/ Fashion
- Food
- Inspiration/ Education
- Holidays / Seasonal
- Humor
- Products
- Travel
- Kids

However, whether you are going to invest a great deal of time in Pinterest or not then adding the 'Pin it' button to your site or images is essential and the first thing you should do. This way anyone who visits your site can 'pin' your images. Many sites have seen an influx of traffic from Pinterest without even having the 'Pin it' button but installing that button will open up yet another source of traffic. To find out whether any of you images from your website have been pinned you can type this URL into your browser http://Pinterest.com/source/YOURSITE.com

Seeing Pinterest from the customers perspective

Before setting up your account it's a really good idea to familiarise yourself with Pinterest and start seeing how and why people are using this platform for their own personal use. Using it for your own personal discovery just for a couple of hours or so will really help to make everything in this book easier to understand and all the strategies and tactics mentioned will be much clearer. The idea is to pick some topics that you are interested in, create some boards, (secret boards if you wish) start following some profiles and start pinning images from websites.

Once you start using it and start enjoying the experience you will see this platform from the perspective of the customer. You will see the ease at which relaxed browsing of visuals converts so easily into sales and see how online communities are built. By doing this hopefully you will see and fully appreciate why this platform is having such a positive impact on businesses. It's a great confidence booster too and the strategies explained in this book will be much clearer and easier to understand. So before you go any further go on have a go.

SETTING UP YOUR ACCOUNT

Pinterest is highly addictive, it is jam packed with amazing images and before you know it you have been dragged into its beauty and a short session has suddenly turned into a 2 hour pinning session! It can be a big time waster which is fine if you are in your own leisure time but if you are using it for your business you need to have clear goals and strategies in place in order to make the most of this platform for your business. Ultimately your goals will be to drive traffic to your website, build your opt-in list, convert followers to buyers and build your brand. These goals are easily achievable with Pinterest but before jumping in and randomly pinning images there is a method to using this social media to reach its full marketing potential and create an outstanding Pinterest experience for your followers. When you start putting the strategies and tactics that you learn into practice you'll be surprised at how quickly it jumps into first place in driving traffic to your website or blog, generating leads and increasing sales.

So lets get started!

Setting up your Pinterest business account

If you already have a personal Pinterest account that you are using for business and you already have a good number of followers then it would be a good idea to convert your account to a business account rather than start from scratch. The Terms and Conditions state that if you wish to use the site for commercial use then you need to set up the account as a business account and agree to their business Terms and Conditions.

To convert your account simply login to your account and then visit the Pinterest for business section found here http://business.pinterest.com/ and click on the text 'convert here'. You will then be taken through the setting up process where you will be asked to select your business type and complete the about section, website name, business name and then you will need to agree to the T&C's.

If you are new to Pinterest or have decided to set up a new account for business you simply visit this URL http://business.pinterest.com/ Setting up your account is very straight forward. You will be asked to select your business type and add your business name and add a username. Your username will become your Pinterest URL , http://pinterest.com/username and you are allowed up to 15 characters. It's a good idea to use your business name as your username, however, if it doesn't fit then you can either use an abbreviation or something that is simple and easy to remember.

You will then be asked to upload your logo or photo. A head shot may be preferable if you are a blogger or a personal brand as often people prefer to connect and follow individuals rather than brands. However for some businesses a logo will be better and will help to promote a more corporate identity. Whatever you choose its advisable to keep it consistent with your brand on other social profiles so your brand is easy to recognise and connect with. Your Pinterest profile picture dimensions are 160×165 pixels.

The 'About' section

The about section is one of the first things users will see when they land on your page and is also a hot spot for search engine optimization. Google ranks Pinterest accounts highly and since the appearance of

Pinterest accounts in search is largely based on the content of profiles, the about section is very important. You have up to 160 characters for this section so make the most of these by using as many keywords from your niche as possible. If you are going to use your brand name then you can personalize your account by adding your name or the names of those who will be managing your account.

Verify your website
Next you will need to verify your website. This establishes a link between your website and Pinterest and confirms that you are the owner of your website and will give you access to your analytics too. To do this simply click on the pencil icon in the top right hand corner of the name box and then enter your web address in the website field and click verify. You can verify with an HTML file or a META tag. Pinterest gives clear instructions on how to do this but if you are still having problems your web designer will be able to do this is five minutes.

Link to your other social media profiles
Make sure you add links to your Facebook and Twitter profiles. Once you have added those and allowed Pinterest to obtain information from these accounts you can post to these sites. You will also be notified when one on your followers joins Pinterest. You can only link to your personal profile on Facebook if you want to link to your Facebook Page then you can do this using an app.

Add the 'Pin it' button to your website
Next you will need to add the 'Pin it' button to your website and next to any images that you want to share. Pinterest gives you the code to embed at www.pinterest.com/about/goodies you can choose from various 'Pin it' or 'Follow' buttons. Now anyone who visits your website will be able to press the 'Pin it' button on your site and then share your content on any of their boards. By viewing your Pinterst analytics you will be able to view how many of your pins have been pinned from your website, how many people saw those pins and how many people clicked through to

your site as a result of seeing those pins. You will be notified every time someone repins one of your pins.

Installing a 'Pin it' button on your browser

To pin directly from your browser simply install Google Chrome and install the 'Pin it' button to your toolbar, once installed you can pin any image from any site and Google Chrome makes it even easier now, you only have to mouse over an image now and you will see the Pin It button.

Installing the 'Pin It' Button to your mobile browser

This is incredibly handy especially if you are using Pinterest to organize your own interests. To add simply follow these steps:

- Open up Safari in iPhone or iPad and go to http://www.pinterest.com
- Add a bookmark by tapping on the icon that looks like a box with an arrow coming out of it.
- **Select 'Bookmark' from the selection of icons and then change the title from Pinterest to 'Pin It' and tap 'Save' on the top right.**
- Tap on the icon that looks like an open book and select 'Edit' and then 'Pin It'
- Below the title, you will see a box to add the bookmark's address. Delete the Pinterest URL and paste the following code:

```
javascript:void((function(d){var %20e=d.createElement('script');e.setAttribute('type','text/javascript');e.setAttribute('charset','UTF-8');e.setAttribute('src','//assets.pinterest.com/js/pinmarklet.js?r='+Math.random()*99999999);d.body.appendChild(e)})(document));
```

Creating a really good looking account

Whether you have decided to convert your existing account or set up a new business account you need to create a really good looking account. When users arrive on your profile it needs to be interesting, eye catching and inviting.

To help get you started here are some Pinterest basics.

Pin Basics

Before you get going and start creating your boards here are some pin basics:

What is a pin?
A pin is a visual bookmark of an image or video. The pin has a description and a link back to the original webpage or blog.

How to pin an image
You can pin an image in three ways:
- **Clicking the 'Pin it' button.** Many sites have a 'Pin it' button. You simply click this and then Pinterest offers you a selection of images from that webpage to pin in a pop up box. Once you have selected the image you can select the board you wish to add it to and then add a description. Pinterest takes the original URL to link the image to. You can install the 'Pin It' button onto the toolbar of your browser by simply going to www.pinterest.com/about/goodies. Once you have installed this you can pin any image from any site.
- **Uploading an image.** You can upload an image from any file on your computer. Simply click on + sign situated on the top right and then '**Upload a Pin**' on the drop down menu. This is very handy if the image does not exist on your website but you still want to pin interesting images.
- **Manually adding a pin.** Instead of using the 'Pin it' button you can manually add the pin by clicking 'Add Pin' on the top right drop down menu and then adding the URL of the page where the image is. You will be offered all the images on that page and then you select the image you want and click 'pin it'.

Repinning an image

If you see an image that you like on Pinterest you can repin that to any of your boards simply by clicking the 'Pin it' button and you can add your own description. That pin that you have repinned will show up in the newsfeed of your followers and this is how your pins can spread virally. This is a similar action to a retweet on Twitter.

A Board

A board is a virtual pin board where you organize your pins by topic. Boards can be secret or public and you can have as many as you like, they are incredibly useful for anyone who wants to organize, keep and find things in one place. Popular collections/boards include: recipes, wedding ideas, films to watch, books to read, gift ideas, home decorating ideas, fashion ideas, inspirational quotes, gardening ideas, interesting articles, and the list goes on and on.

As a business you can use brands to show off your products and anything related to your brand that your audience may be interested in and anything you want associated with your brand. Pinterest is incredibly powerful when it comes to promoting your brand because this is where you can really go to town in visually representing it.

To create a board simply click the **+** symbol and '**Create board**' and then add a name and a description.

Follow

Like Twitter and Facebook you can follow other users on Pinterest and you can either follow profiles or particular boards. You can sign up with Facebook or Twitter which makes it easy to find and follow friends who are already using Pinterest.

Like

You can like any pin without having to follow the profile or board. When you like something on Pinterest it will not appear in your Newsfeed, however the owner of the pin will get notified.

Comment

If you want to leave a comment on Pinterest then you need to click on the pin to enlarge it and then you can leave a comment in the box provided.

Pinterest on Mobile

Pinterest is big on mobile, in fact statistics show that 75% of its usage is coming from mobile. With the mobile app you can pin on the go from anywhere and the app offers a similar Pinterest experience to that which you will find on the web.

The Pinterest Business Blog

Pinterest has produced a blog for businesses and this is a great way to keep up to date with what is going on with Pinterest and the great things that brands are doing on Pinterest and also they will be broadcasting Webinars on the blog. This blog will continually give you new ideas for you to apply and drive your business and you can follow this blog at http://businessblog.pinterest.com/

Chapter Four

Content is King on Pinterest

NOW YOU HAVE set up your profile and added your 'pin it' button(s) to your website you are ready to set up your boards. Whether or not you have an image rich business you will need to create some initial boards in order to give a good visual impression when your potential customers arrive on your profile. Your profile needs to be interesting, eye catching and inviting.

Pinterest is not just about showcasing your products. While your ultimate goal is to sell your products it's also about understanding your customer and finding out what makes them tick. Randomly creating boards that you think may be interesting is not going to work. To be successful in creating the visual experience your audience is looking for you will need to plan the experience you want to create and then how you are going to put your boards together to best promote your products. Later on in this section you will discover some ideas for creating your boards but first you will need to consider and research your target audience and your competition.

Researching your Target Audience

Hopefully by the time you have created your profile you will already have a clear idea of who your ideal customer is. However Pinterest is going to give even more information about your customers which will not only assist you with your marketing on Pinterest but with all your social media platforms.

Never has it been so easy to research what your customers are interested in than with Pinterest. You can literally gain huge insight into what makes they like and what their interests and desires are by simply looking at their boards and seeing what they are pinning and repinning. To find out what your potential customers are interested in, simply type a generic term for your product into the search box and it will bring up all the images relating to that search. If you look under the image you can see how many times it has been repinned and by whom. Simply click on the name of somebody who has repinned that image and it will bring you to the profile of that pinner. You will then see all their boards and what they are interested in.

Here is an example. I typed the term 'wedding flowers' into search and I came up with lots of images of flowers. I picked an image which had been repinned 19 times and then clicked on the name of one of the users who had pinned this image. When I arrived at this particular lady's profile she had 5 boards and these were the titles: 'Love this,' 'Planning our new kitchen,' 'Going to the chapel and we're going...' 'New home inspiration' and 'This year I would like to wear'. That's a huge amount of information about a user and what they are interested in.

This information is like gold and it's worth spending a great deal of time looking around and seeing what your audience are pinning and repinning. Viewing more than a few profiles is going to give you invaluable information and insight into what your audience are looking for before creating your own boards.

Here is a list of questions you should asking yourself about your audience when planning your boards:

Who are the audiences you need to connect with?
Are these audiences using Pinterest?
Are they following your competition on Pinterest?
What are they interested in? What are they pinning?

What are they looking for ?
What sort of topics would appeal to them?
What are the problems they have that they need solving?

Your competition on Pinterest
You can find out a great deal of information about your target audience from your competition as well. See what they are pinning and see what their followers are liking and pinning and repinning. It maybe they are not doing a great job and maybe you will see ways you can do it better. It's definitely worthwhile spending time researching as many of your competitors or other businesses offering similar products.

PREPARING YOUR WEBSITE OR BLOG

The first thing you need to do before producing any fresh content is go back to your blog or website and image check your content and check whether it has a pinnable images. If you do not have images on your website then nothing can be pinned, nothing can be repinned and none of your content has the potential to go viral.

If you are a product based business then you are probably going to have enough material . However, if you do not have an image rich site and you really want to leverage the full power of this platform to drive sales then you are going to need to create your own original content and images to go with that content.

If you already have valuable articles or any valuable content on your site which do not have an image then you need upload a relevant image to the your website or blog so it can be shared on Pinterest. You will also need to decide how you can incorporate these images in your overall board strategy. There are three ways you can create content on Pinterest:

i.) You can repin content
ii.) Pin directly from websites and blogs
iii.) Create your own pins

Each method has its advantages and uses, however research has shown that 80% of content on pinterest is repinned. While this shows how viral and how successful sharing is on Pinterest it also demonstrates the huge opportunity there is for creating fresh content on Pinterest. Like with any social media Pinterest is not the total marketing solution it's another tool to use to drive traffic to your website for sales or to build your opt-in list. Whatever web page you are pinning from, you need to make sure that it is clear where the product can be bought and that your opt-in sign form is prominent with a clear incentive to join.

Creating Outstanding Pins and Boards

As time goes by you will be adding more and more pins and boards to your profile but to get started it's advisable to set up at least 5-10 boards with at least 10 pins on each board. Your aim here is to delight your target audience and create an enjoyable experience for them by giving them what they love. Once you have done your research you will have a good idea what is going to appeal to them.

You may not have too many of your own images to begin with but this is fine as you can pin or repin from other profiles or websites. You can set up some really impressive initial boards with a view to adding your own content at a later date which will add to the experience.

When creating your boards, organization is paramount and you need to think about how you are going to make it as easy as possible for users to find what they are looking for. To create a board simply click the **+Add** at the top next to the Pinterest logo and then click **Create Board.** Here are some tips for creating your boards

Create secret boards
It's good practice to create secret boards and then change them to public when you are ready to go public. This way you can be confident that your boards are ready to publicize. Remember though you cannot go back to

secret once you have gone public.

Themed boards

Organising your boards and making them interest specific is going to be much more effective than just bunching a load of unrelated pins together. Theming your board around a top category is beneficial if you have the relevant products or services.

Naming your boards

Board names are really important and a good unique board name will enhance your Pinterest experience and encourage people to follow you. Users are not usually searching for brands they are searching for topics so you need to be specific when naming your boards. Being inspirational, unique funny and a little bit different is paramount on Pinterest. Board names which are original, unique, quirky or funny have the potential to go viral so this is where you can get really inventive and imaginative. Even businesses that are considered to be quite uninspiring can really get creative and use Pinterest to make their business more interesting and stand out with really interesting board titles and relevant content.

As well as creating names which are interesting and attention grabbing you need to make sure you optimise your board descriptions for search purposes by including the relevant keywords from your niche.

Make the most of your cover images

Make sure you select the best images for your board covers and make sure they are your images if possible. You can change the cover image anytime.

Board organization

It is important to position your most important boards to the top so that when a user lands on your profile they see your best and most relevant content at the top. Boards can be moved and reorganized by simply dragging them into the new position.

CREATIVE IDEAS FOR YOUR BOARDS

With the competition out there on the internet for attention the only way you are going to win is by inspiring your audience with high quality images and content on Pinterest. You may be wondering how you are going to consistently produce and display compelling images to your audience on a regular basis for the foreseeable future. However once you have picked your topics of interest you will surprised how one idea lead will lead to another and you will be able to find ideas for numerous boards and images to create and pin.

Product boards

If you are an image rich business or have tangible products for sale then the first board you will want to create is one with your products. Depending how many products you have, you may wish to create more than one board. You could create one board with all your images included and then also include certain product images on other boards that may be related to other board topics. If you have images of your products actually being used by customers then these can be very effective for promoting a type of lifestyle.

Business resources that your clients will love

If you are selling to other businesses, then your audience will find anything to do with helping them in their business of value. Posting informative content about your subject is invaluable, this will help you to stand out as a thought leader and expert in your field. If your content is valuable and useful then your followers are likely to keep coming back for more and are likely to share your content too. Remember your audience are looking to find and share valuable content with their friends and customers too and will want to be associated with any compelling content you create. Creating a board of useful tips is incredibly effective especially if the original source of the pin is from your site or one of your landing pages with a picture of your product or an incentive and form to join your opt-in list.

A Board to Help
Whatever you are selling then there will be a subject or subjects that will help your audience. Maybe you are in real estate and then a board about how to get your house ready for a sale would be very useful. If you are in fashion then you can create a board about how to accessorise or maybe fashion tips or even tips about color matching. Instructions on how to do things is very big on Pinterest. If you can create boards to help others and include pins with instructions on how to do certain things which appeal to your target audience you are probably onto a winner with regard to the viral sharing of your content. This can be incredibly powerful for your branding.

Relatable Content Board
Relatable content is one of the best types of content and one of the most shared types of content. Relatable content is anything that your target audience can relate to and identify with, it's when your audience sees a piece of content and immediately thinks, "Yes, I can relate to that and this is exactly the way I feel when this happens". It's incredibly powerful because it means that your content is communicating to your audience and showing that you understand and empathise with them and you feel their pain or joy. With relatable content you are communicating with them on quite a deep level which all helps to build relationships and trust. This is why 'Someecards' is so successful, most of their content is relatable.

Product user boards
Ask your customers to pin pictures of themselves using your product or what they have produced using your products. This could be anything from nail polish to paint.

Seasonal boards
Creating boards for your brand based on the seasons are a great way to market your products, for example: Christmas Day, Mothers Day, Fathers

Day, Easter, etc. Make sure you position your seasonal boards so they are at the top at the right time of year, and when they are out of season then position them at the bottom.

Collaborative boards
Collaborative boards are boards that you invite other users to pin to. The benefits of a collaborative board are endless. It's a great way to increase exposure as it introduces you to the followers of those you are collaborating with and helps to build relationships and follower numbers. Bloggers can invite other bloggers, businesses can invite their employees. You may wish to invite users to pin about a common interest to encourage networking. If you are promoting a joint event or fund raiser, creating a collaborative board can increase your reach no end.

To create a collaborative board you simply create the board and then click 'Edit' and you will be able to add the email address or the username of those people you wish to invite. To invite users to join a collaborative board you need to follow them and then send them an invite, however be careful not to spam other users by sending more than one invite. To encourage collaboration leave a comment in the description field to say that you welcome other pinners and to ask interested users to leave a comment with their user name so you can send them an invite. You can also let your followers know that you are doing this on your other social networks. If you do create collaborative boards then you will need to monitor the content on the board carefully, since any pin that is added will appear on your feed.

'How to' boards
Because of the visual nature of Pinterest a series of 'how to' images can make a very effective board. You can also pin tutorials and Webinars. For example, if you are selling toys for children then maybe you could make visuals about how a child can make a model or toy. If you are selling produce or an ingredient then a 'how to' image about how to make something with that ingredient is an obvious winner.

Testimonial boards

If people are saying good things about your products and services then pinning those comments will create credibility and social proof for your business.

Infographics and graphs

People love statistics especially if they are portrayed in an easy to understand way with eye catching images. Infographics and graphs are really popular on Pinterest particularly with B2B businesses, they are very shareable and have great viral potential too.

Inspiring and motivational boards

The truth is everyone has a bad day sometimes and needs a little bit of motivation or cheering up. A motivational quote will help to lift your audience and can really help you to connect with them. If you know what your audience wants, what they aspire to and what their frustrations are then it is likely that you will be able to motivate them by posting content which inspires them. These types of post are also very shareable especially if put together with a colourful and inspiring image like a cartoon or photo.

Event boards

You can create boards about exhibitions and events in your industry and also publicize your own events by displaying images from an event that has already taken place. Collaborative boards work very well with events and you can get different people pinning their perspective of an event.

History boards

A history board of your business and how it has developed through the years can add huge interest, credibility and authenticity to your profile. You could also create a board with the history of your industry.

Entertaining/amusing content

Social media is all about being social and having fun, and people love sharing funny stuff. Even if you did not create it yourself but you think it is going to appeal to your target audience then share it. The aim here is to amuse and entertain your audience, humor is a winner all round and not only does humor break down barriers it is also more likely to be liked and shared. Funny stuff is one of the top ten categories on Pinterest.

Color boards

Organising your boards into colors can be very effective especially if you are involved in design, fashion or home style. Creating color themed boards with products that compliment your products, are a great way to grab your audience's attention.

Your current content

If you do not have your own tangible products as such but do have articles or other types of written content then you will need to pin all these. Make sure you create interesting and unique images for any of your content which will encourage your blog visitors to pin your image.

Complimentary product boards

Create boards with products that compliment your product. For example, you may be selling laptops, so pinning anything related to laptops like lap top cases will increase your reach on Pinterest. If you own hotel then you can pin information about places of interest that are local to your hotel, you may even get those places reciprocating and pinning your hotel or establishment. If you are a wedding cake maker you could pin local wedding suppliers and hopefully they will reciprocate too.

Video Boards

If you have a YouTube channel then these videos are ideal for pinning. Make sure you use the word video in the title of your board. Simply copy the short code for your video from YouTube (click share and YouTube will give you a short URL to copy) and then paste it into the '**Add Pin**' URL Box. There are so many ideas for videos, 'how to' videos, product demonstrations, talking head videos and funny videos. Creating a collaborative board for videos is an excellent way to share content and gain new followers. People are always looking for ways to publicize their videos. You could also create a board where people have submitted videos for a competition where they are using your product.

Behind the scenes
Giving your audience a behind the scenes view of your business helps to keep you business and brand looking real and authentic and adds human interest. People love to see the production process and watch how the product was made before they buy.

Employee boards
An introduction to your team will help to humanise your brand and adds a personal touch. Followers will have a sense that they have already met your staff, particularly if you include videos. It also shows your followers that you value them and want them to get to know your business in a more personal way. If you have news about your employees and the great things they are doing, then post it. Maybe they have been involved in a fundraiser or they have won an employee of the month award.

Non Industry Boards
Creating boards about other popular topics can help to widen your reach, but be careful here as you may just be wasting time on an audience that is not actually interested in your products.

Customer success boards
Highlighting your customers' successes or including case studies on a board is a great way of displaying social proof. You also keep your customers happy by giving them free promotion and they are very likely to share your pin on one of their boards so you reach their followers too.

Local boards
If you are a local business then pinning other businesses or attractions in

the area is a very good idea. If for instance you are a florist, then pinning images of local wedding venues and other wedding suppliers in the area is a great way to create interest around your whole subject. It also attracts the attention of these other suppliers to your business.

To help you give you ideas for boards and see what other brands are doing Pinterest has put a page together made up of brands who have been successful on Pinterest. You can view these at this URL http://business.pinterest.com/success-stories/

Creative Ideas for Pins

The opportunities and ideas for creating pins are endless but here are a few ideas to get you started:

Product images
Make sure your products photos are really beautiful. It may be worthwhile to get these done by a professional if you haven't done already, to really help emphasize and highlight the beauty and uniqueness of your product.

Step by step images
A tall image made up of three or four images showing step by step instructions or the development of a product are really effective and very popular.

Inspirational or motivational images
An inspirational quote or motivational tip set in a beautiful picture is always a winner on Pinterest. If you are using images then making the best use of the space available is crucial. www.pinstamatic.com is a great tool for creating this type of image.

Pictures that make you go Awww!
Images of cute animals and children are a real winner on Pinterest.

Before and after images
These are particularly effective for creatives who do makeovers, like interior designers, hairdressers, beauticians and stylists.

Trending topics
Creating pins relating to trending topics is an obvious choice especially if they relate to your niche. You can find out what is trending on Pinterest with www.repinly.com where you will find a huge amount of information about the most popular pinners and pins.

Offers and competitions
Creating attention grabbing images for any of your latest offers or competitions that you are running on Pinterest or any other social networks will really help to increase your reach. Pinterest is a great way to get the message out about the special offers you have running, but you will need to be careful not to post them too often or they just appear like advertising and bad noise in your audience's news feed. You need to make sure that what you are offering is of real value, that it is exclusive to your followers and you are offering them a deadline to redeem the offer.

Above all be unique
Pinterest users love new fresh interesting and original content, so if you can be unique in your pin creation and put your own stamp on your pins, this will go along way in creating content that is more likely to get shared and go viral.

CREATING YOUR PINS
Once you have a good idea of the boards you wish to create you can start your own. There are a wealth of tools, apps and websites than can assist you with creating amazing pins. This is where you have the potential to create pins that may go viral and suddenly you may have thousands of eyeballs looking at your product or brand. Here are some tips for creating pins:

Image Size

You can pin JPG, PNG or GIF image files. Pinterest does not limit the vertical size of images but the maximum horizontal width size is 554 pixels and anything over that will be resized. The minimum size for an image is 84 Pixels. When pinning from other websites the minimum image size is 100 X 200 pixels. According to research tall images are more likely to get repinned, however it's a good idea to keep height of images under 5000 pixels so the user does not have to scroll down as it is then unlikely that they will scroll back up to comment, like or repin.

Image Quality

Since Pinterest is all about the visual experience then image quality is really important. Because there are so many creatives on Pinterest the standard of images is extremely high, so any images that you pin need be of a very high quality in order to compete. Most smart phones will have good cameras but you need to make sure the light is right and the image is clear and not blurry.

Watermark your image

Watermarking your image not only promotes your brand but also helps to protect you from image theft. It doesn't have to be a large watermark and can be placed in the bottom left or right corner so not to spoil the main picture. Sites like www.watermark.com let you generate watermarks for your images for free. Image theft is always going to be a problem and although you cannot completely stop it you can take steps which will deter the majority from trying.

Stock Photography

Sites like www.shutterstock.com istockphoto.com and www.bigstockphoto.com provide a huge selection of photos on any subject. Make sure you read the terms and conditions with regard to whether or not the images can be used on Pinterest. Some of these sites also offer photo editing tools so you can add effects and text to images.

Use images from photo sharing sites
Photo sharing sites like www.flickr.com and compfight.com offer a great selection of images that are free. Make sure you select images with the Attribution licence and also credit the photographer.

Text on Graphics & Photo Editing
Adding text to graphics is one of the most effective ways to get your images repinned. A good image itself is eye catching but sometimes by adding text you can clarify exactly what the pin is all about and pinners appear to love this. Photoshop is the obvious choice for doing all sorts of wonderful things to images but if you are not an expert then there are other image editing sites like www.picmonkey.com and www.canva.com which are incredibly easy to use and create an extremely professional result.

Infographics
Infographics are the latest sharing craze on Pinterest and other social networks. They have great viral potential and can really shout out your brand particularly if you use your corporate colours. Simply type 'Infographic tool' into Google search and a whole host of different sites will come up to help create infographics.

Pin your videos
You can pin all your videos. YouTube videos are easily pinned by simply using the 'pin it' button. Pinterest supports YouTube and Vimeo.

Online graphic design & marketing services
Sites like Fivver.com which is an online services marketplace, offer inexpensive graphic design and marketing services. This incredibly useful site offers services all starting from $5 including logo design, caricatures, cartoons and other many other design services.

Online pin creation tools
Sites like www.pinstamatic.com and www.pinwords.com offer free tools

for creating instant pins. These tools make Pinterest possible for those of us who are more creatively challenged! You can create quotes in different styles, add text to your images and create sticky note images. Studio Design is an iPhone app which has different filters, fonts and shapes to enhance your images and you can upload them while on the go. You can also create a pin of your location which is linked to Google maps and create a pin of your website or your Twitter profile. Another handy pin creator is Someecards which lets you create your own card.

Be camera ready
Once you adopt the photo mindset on an everyday basis you will start to notice all sorts of photo opportunities within your business and outside. Taking your own photos not only saves you money it also gives you the unique fresh content that pinners will love. As you get used to Pinterest you will find it is all about discovery. Be on the lookout for interesting things that will inspire your audience.

Faces
Iimages without human faces get shared more times than those with faces.

Be colourful
Colour images are more likely to be repinned than black and white images.

Pin Orientation
Images with vertical orientation perform better than horizontal.

Be authentic
Users on Pinterest seem to prefer backgrounds that are real rather than objects which have been superimposed on artificial backgrounds.

ADDING DESCRIPTIONS TO YOUR PINS
It's very important to add good descriptions to all your pins. With every

pin you have the opportunity to add a description of up to 500 characters even if you are repinning an image. Every description area is prime real estate for your business. The optimum length for a pin description is probably between 100 and 200 characters. If it is under 140 it can be tweeted too! You can add your own descriptions or you can quickly autofill the description with the description from the website you pinned the image from. To do this simply highlight the text you wish to copy and then click the pin it button and you will find the text in the description box which saves time.

Optimising your pin descriptions

To get the most out of you pins you will need to take the following into consideration when writing your descriptions:

- **Write for your audience** What is really important is that the image description is interesting and you can write why you feel your pin is interesting. The main priority is to get your visitors so interested that they want to find out more and visit your website. You can be quite inventive with descriptions and a good description that outlines benefits of a product or tells a story can really capture the attention of the audience.
- **Keywords in descriptions** You will need to optimise all your descriptions for Pinterest search by including keywords from your niche. If you are a local business it will be important to add your town or city. This will also work well for Google and Bing Search.
- **Include Price information** According to research, pins with price tags get more likes, so adding prices is definitely a good idea. People naturally want to know if they can buy it and how much it is. You can add prices to all your images by just adding the currency sign. Once you add a price, your products automatically get added to the gift section and the price will be added to the top right hand corner of the image.
- **Add a Call to action.** Including a call to action is essential. You can include this in the image or in the description. Statistics show that images with a call to action result in 80% more interaction.

Examples are 'click here' for more information' or 'Feel free to repin this image' or 'repin this'
- **Add your descriptions to repins** It's good practice to create your own descriptions for images that you repin as it can give your perspective relating to your business.
- **Keywords on your web page** It is really important that if you are pinning from your own website then the page you are pinning from contains the relevant and similar keywords to that of your description. Pinterest seems to take this into consideration in their search results and they obviously do this so that users receive the best search experience and are taken to relevant web pages.
- **File names** It's always a good idea to be as descriptive as possible in the actual file name of the image for search purposes.

BEST PINNING PRACTICES

Pin at least once a day Try and pin or repin at least once a day so you can give your followers fresh content in their feed.

Space out your pins. When you post try not to flood the stream otherwise this can overwhelm your followers especially if it's just more of the same thing. Flooding the stream not only looks like blatant self promotion, it's boring and takes away from the unique Pinterest experience of variety and discovery and doing this will lose you followers. Hootsuite's app, ViralTag, is an excellent tool for scheduling pins you find online but you cannot schedule repins or upload original pins.

Be authentic

Use your pins to show your brands values and your brands vision, personality and what is important to your brand. Pinterest is incredibly powerful when it comes to creating, developing and promoting your brand. You also need to be careful not to pin or repin anything that does not fit in with your branding.

Avoid blatant self promotion
Simply pushing your products and services all the time will not work. When creating pins keep in mind the lifestyle you are trying to promote with your products or services. You can create much more interest by pinning images from other sources.

Do not link pins to affiliate links
Under Pinterest terms and conditions you cannot link directly to affiliate links, however you can embed links to your own website or blog and then link your pins to those pages.

Download the Pinterest iPhone and Android app
If you're an iPhone user, the free Pinterest app lets you pin pictures with your location, directly from your phone.

Time Management
Like any of the social networks Pinterest takes time and it is easy to get dragged into the site and spend literally hours and hours browsing the interesting material available. Once you have set up your initial boards you will need to allocate a certain amount of time each day and then try and keep to that, so you do not waste too much time. Setting a timer is a good idea.

HOW TO USE RICH PINS

Rich pins are pins that allow retailers to add extra information to the images that people pin. There are five different types of rich pin, Product Pin, Place Pins, Article Pins, Recipe Pins and Movie Pins.
- **Place Pins** include a map, address and phone number
- **Article Pins** include headline, author and story description
- **Product Pins** include pricing, availability and where to buy. Pinners also get notified when an item drops in price
- **Recipe Pins** include ingredients, cooking times and serving information and recipe search filters help pinners to find the recipes they are looking for

- **Movie Pins** include information about ratings, cast members and reviews

To get started with rich pins you will need to prepare your website with metatags and then get your Rich Pins validated and then apply to get them approved on Pinterest. You probably want to get a developer to help you if you are not technical. For more information you can visit this page https://developers.pinterest.com/rich_pins/

CHAPTER FIVE

BUILDING YOUR AUDIENCE ON PINTEREST

LIKE ANY OTHER social media network Pinterest is a traffic source and a tool to find new customers. Once you have created your initial boards you will be ready to find and build your audience so that you will be able to do the following:

- Drive traffic to your website
- Promote and sell your products
- Build your opt-in list
- Increase exposure to your products
- Build your brand

Here are some strategies to building your followers on Pinterest:

Install the Pinterest follow button on your website

Make sure you have installed a Pinterest follow button on your website and also install 'Pin it' buttons next to the products on your site as well, if possible. There is still a concern amongst pinners about copyright and about whether or not you are allowed to pin images, so making your website visitors aware that they are welcome to pin your images will go a long way to get people to share your images. You can make it obvious to your visitors by including a call to action, for example, ' Feel free to pin'. You can find buttons at this link www.pinterest.com/about/goodies where you can choose from a selection of widgets to embed on your site including: the pin it button, follow button, pin widget, profile widget and board widget which lets you display up to thirty of your favorites board's latest pins.

Connect your Facebook and Twitter accounts

When you joined Pinterest you may have linked your Twitter and your personal Facebook profile. If you have done this then you will be notified whenever one of your friends joins Pinterest. You can choose to share your Pins on Twitter and Facebook every time you add a pin you can click on the pin to share it. This will increase your reach through your friends, but not a good idea if you are pinning regularly, as it may put your Facebook friends off.

Announce your presence on your other social networks
Create a post for Facebook, Twitter, Google + and any other social networks announcing you are on Pinterest and invite people to follow you.

Select a Pinner of the month
Selecting a 'Pinner of the month' is an incredibly powerful way to encourage pinners to pin and repin your content on Pinterest. This not only helps to grow your reach on Pinterest but also helps to grow your followers. The reason this is so powerful is pinners will be desperate to win that spot as they will gain huge publicity among your followers if they get picked as your 'Pinner of the Month' and in turn you will gain huge exposure amongst their followers. It's a win win for both parties.

Win 'Pinner of the Month'
If you are a personal brand then winning a' Pinner of the Month' competition could offer you huge exposure. Make sure you pick a brand that has the right audience for your brand and is not directly in competition with you.

Email your contacts
Invite your current customers or the people who have joined your opt-in list. Remember every follower you gain on Pinterest has the potential increase your reach by drawing in their contacts and more like minded users with similar interests and therefore helps grow your following.

Cross promote with friends.
If you have friends on Pinterest then ask if they can repin some of your pins on their boards and offer to do the same for them.

Use search to find your target audience
By using the search facility you will be able to find your target audience on Pinterest. Simply type your term into search and it will bring up the images relating to that term, under that image you will see details about how many times an image has been pinned and by who. By following either their profile or one of their boards the user will be notified. Going out of your way to repin their images especially if they are the actual source of the image rather than repinning what they have repinned will really bring your profile to their attention. If you do not want to be too overwhelmed in your feed by too many pins from the same user then following just one of their boards may be better.

Repinning and sharing
Everyone is aiming for repins so if you are helping others out by repinning their content it is going to draw attention to your brand and they are more likely to take interest in your content. This is one area where the reciprocation rule works very well on Pinterest. Engaging with content will also draw attention to you and your brand and you will find that people will click on your profile to find out who you are and you may very well end up with another follower. The more you share the more others will see your actions. Repinning is one of the most social activities on Pinterest, it's how users build their network of followers and works especially well if your business is B2B. Other businesses will appreciate that you are promoting their product by repinning and this is how you can start to build a really good community.

Liking other pins
Liking is also a really good way to connect and draw attention to your brand. Maybe you don't want to repin because a pin doesn't fit in with your brand or any of your boards but you can still like it.

Commenting on pins

Commenting on pins is a really excellent way of engaging with the community. Once you start interacting you will create interest in your own content too, other people will see your comments and may be drawn to come and have a look at one of your boards. The more you participate and get involved the more you will grow your following which makes for more eyeballs on your content. Be careful not to comment too much at one time, Pinterest may consider this as spammy behaviour and suspend your commenting privileges.

Comment on popular pins

This section can be found here http://www.pinterest.com/popular/ You need to make sure you are writing thoughtful comments and not too many for the reason mentioned above.

Contribute to other boards

This is a great way to get noticed . Contributing to popular boards with interesting pins will put you in front of even more users and help contribute to your follow count.

Mention / Tag other users

You can draw attention to people and your profile by tagging them and they will be sent an email notifying them. Simply add the @ sign before their profile name. This really helps to build rapport in your community. You can recommend a pin to someone, start a conversation or ask questions.

Advertising on Pinterest

Pinterest are now introducing Promoted Pins. Promoted Pins work in a similar way to Facebook promoted posts and basically advertisers can pay to get their pins to show up higher under certain categories. The platform is currently experimenting with certain businesses this but will soon be rolled out to other businesses in due course.

CREATING A CONTEST ON PINTEREST

One way of building your following is to run a Pinterest competition. Competitions can also help you to grow your opt-in list, drive traffic to your website, promote a new product and build your brand. If you need inspiration then type the words competition, or, contest, into Pinterest search and have a look at some of the competitions currently running. Pinterest has tightened up their terms and conditions regarding promotions and this is most probably because they want to preserve the Pinterest experience which is all about discovery, creativity and interests. If you want to create a contest or competition it's probably a very good idea to use a third party as they will ensure that the terms and conditions are met. Here are the steps you need to take to create your competition or contest:

Decide on the type of competition

The type of contest you wish to run will depend on your goal and whether you wish to increase your following, build your opt in list, increase exposure or promote a particular product. Creative contests tend to gain more engagement while sweepstakes may gain you more followers. Here are a few ideas about the types of contest you may wish to run:

- **Photo or video contest** Create a board which allows your entrants to upload an image or video. Ask your audience to submit their videos or photos of them using your product. This is great for creating engagement and buzz and entrants will often want to share and shout about their own creations with their friends and followers which will increase your brand reach even further.
- **Pin Now Contest** Simply ask your entrants to create a board with the board name you have chosen and ask them to choose their favorite products from your website. To administer this you will need to create a landing page to administer the contest and ask entrants to complete an entry form and share their board

URL on the form. Alternatively you can ask them to pin just one of their favorite images from your site and complete an entry form. **NB** Under Pinterest terms and conditions you cannot ask entrants to pin something from a predefined selection of pins. You should not require a minimum number of pins and you cannot name your competition 'pin it to win it'.

- **Sweepstakes** Sweepstakes are a great way to build your opt-in list. Rafflecopter.com lets you set up contests in minutes and offers an easy entry process.
- **Blog or website contest** If your competition is all about launching a new product you may want to simply send your audience to a landing page where they find out about your product and then have to answer a question and leave a comment on your website or blog. (Not on Pinterest as one of their Terms and Conditions states: 'Don't Encourage spammy behaviour, such as asking participants to comment'.)

Whatever the type of competition you choose to run be sure to keep it simple and easy to enter, the easier it is to enter the more entrants you will get. Also make sure your competition's landing page is optimised for mobile and tablets. You can do this by using a third party app like www.wishpond.com or www.woobox.com or www.shortstack.com These apps also help to keep track of entries, assist in selecting a winner and ensure that you keep within the Pinterest terms and conditions.

Decide on a significant prize

The prize needs to reflect the effort that you expect your audience to put in and obviously the bigger the prize the more people will enter. Also you need to pick a prize that will appeal to your target audience so when they do start following they will actually be interested in your pins and engage with your content. The 'Win an iPad' competitions can draw large numbers of followers but they don't necessarily attract the right audience and promote your product. To keep your audience happy it's also really good to give your entrants a reward for entering like a small gift or maybe money off coupon.

Create a landing page
Create your contest landing page on your website or blog with a description of the contest, entry instructions, competition entry form, terms and conditions and closing date. You will need to be clear how you will be picking the winner.

Create your competition pin & description
You will need to create a compelling image to promote your contest on Pinterest. Adding clear title text to the image and the description field promoting contest will help to increase the numbers of entrants. Your description needs to clearly describe what the competition is all about, what the prize is and when the closing date is. Including a date will also help to get your contest found as people may well enter a search terms like 'contest September 20_ _. Try and include as many keywords as possible including words like competition, sweepstake, win, giveaway , promotion.

Add a value
If your prize has a monetary value then add this in the description with currency sign and it will then show up in the top right of the image.

Promote your contest
You will need to create some buzz to draw attention for your Pinterest contest. Here are some ideas how you can do this:
- Invite your subscribers from your opt in list
- Announce your contest on your other social networks
- Create a board for other peoples competitions as well as your own to help drive traffic to yours, example 'September contest on Pinterest'
- Add your contest pin at different times of the day and create different images of the prizes to promote the same contest
- Promote on your blog or website

- Use Facebook advertising
- Create some information about your competition in print for the customers who visit your business to take away. This could literally be just a note on a receipt

Pick a winner

You can run a sweepstake and choose a winner from all the entries. www.random.org offers a service that selects winners of competitions. Alternatively you can appoint a panel of judges to pick the best board or use another third party contest app.

Pin a picture of the winner or winning pin

This is a great way to make your contest look authentic especially if you are planning to launch another one. You can also include the information in the pin to introduce yet another contest. People are very suspicious about contests so by doing this you will give users the confidence that the contest is real and they are more likely to enter.

Delete the contest when it's over

There is nothing worse than visiting a page with an out of date contest, it's disappointing for your followers and will leave them with a negative feeling about your business. Make sure you delete the pin when it is over or replace the content on the web page with a new contest or a picture of the winner.

Check on competition terms

This is a big one. Make sure you are aware of the rules for contests in your own state, region or country and make sure you read Pinterest guidelines about marketing and the do's and don'ts for running a contest http://business.pinterest.com/en/brand-guidelines Here are a list of Don'ts taken from that page;
- Suggest that Pinterest sponsors or endorses you or the contest.
- Require people to add Pins from a selection—let them add what they like.
- Make people Pin your contest rules. This is a biggie.

- Run sweepstakes where each Pin, board, like or follow represents an entry.
- Encourage spammy behaviour, such as asking participants to comment.
- Ask people to vote with Pins, boards, or likes.
- Overdo it: contests can get old fast.
- Require a minimum number of Pins. One is plenty.
- Call your contest a "Pin it to win it" contest.

If you use Pinterest as part of a contest or sweepstakes, you are responsible for making sure it complies with all legal requirements. This includes writing the official rules, offer terms and eligibility requirements (eg: age and residency restrictions), and complying with marketing regulations (eg: registration requirements and regulatory approvals). These rules can vary from place to place, so please work with a lawyer or other expert to make sure you're in compliance. You should also always comply with Pinterest's Terms of Service.

Chapter Six

Measuring and Monitoring your Results on Pinterest

MEASURING AND MONITORING your results and performance against your original goals and objectives on a continual basis is essential. This is where many businesses go wrong, they carry on aimlessly posting content without checking to see what is working and what is not. Then after 6 months or a year they wonder why their campaign is making no positive difference at all.

When you measure your results you will discover so much information that will allow you to steer your campaign in the right direction to achieve those SMART goals and objectives and also to stop anything that is not working.

When you initially work out strategies and tactics for your campaign, you will be estimating what you need to do to achieve your goals and objectives. However as your campaign runs you will see exactly what you need to do to achieve you original goals. For example, you may need to change the types of posts you make to increase engagement and reach. Perhaps you need to increase the number of competitions you run to increase the number of opt-in subscribers. This is what it is all about, making your campaign work for you by constantly measuring your success against the goals set and then adjusting your strategies accordingly in order to achieve the results.

To help you measure your results Pinterest offers very good analytics and also you can use Google Analytics. There are other tools available on the net but these two should be sufficient.

Pinterest Analytics

With the launch of the new Pinterest analytics tool you can now measure the success of your marketing efforts and really see whether it is working for your business. You can see which pins are getting shared, how many pins are getting pinned from your website and you can learn about what pinners like.

Once you have verified your website you can access analytics on your business account for free. Analytics is accessible from the top right in the drop down menu. If you already have an active account then you need to make sure you switch to the new look which is situated at the bottom of the drop down menu .

Pinterest analytics will help you understand how pinners are engaging with your content. Once you are into your analytics dashboard you will be able to access all sorts of useful information.

- **Pins** The average number of things pinned from your website.
- **Pinners** The average number of unique people who have pinned from your website.
- **Repins** The average number of times pins from your website have been repinned.
- **Repinners** The average number of unique people who repinned your pins on Pinterest.
- **Impressions** The average number of times your pins appeared in feed and search for boards on the web.
- **Reach** The daily number of unique people who saw your pins on Pinterest.
- **Clicks** The average number of clicks to your website from Pinterest.
- **Visitors** The average number of unique people who visit your site from Pinterest.
- **+/- %** Percent increase or decrease from your current date range

to a previous date range.
You can also see your websites most recent pins and most repinned pins and most clicked pins.

GOOGLE ANALYTICS

Google Analytics will be able to give you detailed information about the impact Pinterest is having on your business.

Google Analytics Social Reports
Google Analytics provides advance reports that let you track the effectiveness of your campaign with the following social reports:

The Overview Report
This report lets you see at a glance how much conversion value is generated from social channels. It compares all conversions with those resulting from social.

The Conversions Report
The Conversions Report helps you to quantify the value of social and shows conversion rates and the monetary value of conversions that occurred due to referrals from Pinterest and any of the other social networks. Google Analytics can link visits from Pinterest with the goals you have chosen and your E - commerce transactions. To do this you will need to configure your goals in Google Analytics which is found under **'Admin'** and then **'Goals'**. Goals in Google Analytics let you measure how often visitors take or complete a specific action and you can either create goals from the templates offered or create your own custom goals. The Conversions report can be found in the Standard Reporting tab under Traffic Sources > Social > Conversions.

The Networks Referral Report The Networks Referral report tells you how many visitors the social networks have referred to your website and shows you how many pageviews,visits, the duration of the visits and the average number of pages viewed per visit. From this information you can determine which network referred the highest quality of traffic.

Data Hub Activity The Data Hub activity report shows how people are engaging with your site on the social networks. You can see the most recent URL's that were shared, how they were shared and what was said.

The social visitors flow report This report displays the initial paths that your visitors took from social sites through your site and where they exited.

The landing pages report This report displays engagement metrics for each URL. These include pageviews, average visit duration and pageviews and pages viewed per visit.

The Trackbacks Report The Trackback report shows you which sites are linking to your content and how many visits those sites are sending to you. This can help you to work out which sort of content is the most successful so you can create similar and also helps you to build relationships with those who are constantly linking to your content.

Tracking Custom Campaigns with Google Analytics

Google Analytics lets you create URL's for custom campaigns for website tracking. This helps you identify which content is the most effective in driving visitors to your website and landing pages. For instance you may want to see which particular links are sending you the most traffic from Pinterest or you may want to see which links in an email are sending you the most traffic. Custom Campaigns let you measure this and see what is and what is not working by letting you add parameters to the end of your URL. You can either add you own or use the URL Builder.

To do this simply type 'URL builder' into Google and click on the first result. The URL builder form will only appear if you are signed into Google. You then need to add the URL, that you want to track, to the form provided and then complete the fields and click 'Submit.' You will then need to shorten the URL with bit.ly or goo.gl/ . Once you have set these up you can track the results within Google Analytics.

CHAPTER SEVEN

BUILDING YOUR BRAND THROUGH PINTEREST

YOUR MAIN AIM through this whole process is going to be to connect, capture, and convert your prospects through your website or blog, Pinterest, and through other social networks, and this involves the following:

- **Connect:** Your product needs to be the connection between your prospect and what they need so the first thing you need to do is connect those two things. In order to do this you need to identify who they are, find them out of all the millions of people on the Internet, and then connect with them by offering them something they want or need.
- **Capture:** Once you have found them you need to capture them on your website, blog, Pinterest, or any other social media platforms. This is so you can continue your relationship with them either by email or through Pinterest and continue to communicate your brand message. To do this you need to offer them some sort of incentive so you can capture their name and email address.
- **Convert:** When you have captured your prospect you need to convert them into a paying customer by nurturing them and continuing to build a relationship by offering them the content they want through email and Pinterest and then moving them toward signing up for a special or exclusive offer.

To achieve this successfully you are going to need to have a well-defined brand, and that brand needs to be communicated through everything you do or say through Pinterest , your website, blog, and your email campaign.

Whether you are a one person small business, a large corporation, or an organization, your brand is one of the most important attributes of your business. Your brand is what you want your prospects and customers to respect, trust, and fall in love with so they will buy and continue to buy your products and services. Your brand is what is going to set you apart from any other business and what will give your business the competitive edge.

Never has there been a better time for your business to build your brand and communicate your brand message to your target audience than through Pinterest . Your brand is the main ingredient for success, and Pinterest is giving you the channel to communicate it. You can literally communicate with your audience every day. If you get it right and connect the right brand experience with the right target audience, you are onto an all-around winner.

It may be that you have a well-established brand already or maybe you have not created your brand yet or it just needs some tweaking or fine tuning. Maybe you are not exactly sure what your brand is, or maybe you feel it needs a complete overhaul. Whatever your situation is, you need to know that your brand is going to underpin your whole Pinterest campaign, and it needs to be strong, clear, well-defined, and consistent. Once defined, your business is going to create it, be it, communicate it, display it, picture it, speak it, promote it, and most of all, be true to it. This chapter is going to take you through everything you need know and do to define and create your brand so you can get into the hearts and minds of your target audience by communicating the right message and brand experience.

There are many definitions of the word brand but this is the one I like best because it incorporates pretty much all the necessary information you will need to help you to define your own brand.

Brand, the definition

Your brand is more than a name, symbol, or logo. It is your commitment and your promise to your customer. Your brand is the defined personality of either yourself as an individual brand or your product, service, company, or organization. It's what sets you apart and differentiates your business from your competition and any other business. Your brand is created and influenced by your vision and everything you stand for, including people, visuals, culture, style, perception, words, messages, PR, opinions, news media, and, especially, social media.

Why is your brand so important to your business?

Branding is important because it helps you and your business build and create powerful and lasting relationships by communicating everything you want to say about your product or service to your prospects and customers. A strong brand encourages loyalty and will ultimately create a strong customer base and increase your sales by doing the following:

- Demonstrating to your prospects and customers that you are professional and committed to offering them what you promise
- Making your business easily recognizable
- Creating a clear distinction from your competition
- Making your business memorable
- Creating an emotional attachment with your audience
- Helping to create trust
- Helping to build customer loyalty and repeat custom
- Creating a valuable asset which will be financially beneficial if you sell your business
- Creating a competitive advantage

To do all the above you are going to have to find a way to get into the hearts and minds of your customers so they will ultimately buy and continue to buy your products or services. Before launching your campaign and setting up profiles, posting content, and engaging, you will need to have a clear picture of exactly what your brand is or what you want your brand to be. You will need to define exactly how your brand is perceived now, how you want your brand to be perceived, where your business fits into the market, who your target audience is, and how you want your business to develop in the future.

To do this you need a deep understanding of your business and the people who are going to be most interested in your products and how you are going to serve them. When it comes to defining your ideal target audience, you need to work out which of your products are the most popular and which are the most profitable so you can focus your efforts in finding and connecting with the right audience and then creating the right brand experience for them.

Your Vision/Your Story

If you want to create a strong brand, one of the first things you need to do is create a clear visual picture of how you see your business now and in the future. This is about daring to see what your business could be without constraints or limitations.

This exercise will not only help you to work out what you want to achieve financially and creatively, but it also makes you focus on what really matters and will help you to create your own unique voice and story. This is incredibly important when it comes to your branding as this is what is going to make your business stand out from others and give you that edge.

To do this, you need to get away from all distractions and think about how you would like to see your business grow and develop in the next three years. This is more than just putting a mission statement together. This is about your core business beliefs, why you are doing it, what you want your business to be, and how you want to be perceived in your market. To help you do this you will need to ask yourself the following questions and record your answers:

- Why did you originally start your business or why are you starting a business?
- How did your original business idea come about?
- What changes are you looking to make in peoples' lives?
- What are you hoping to achieve?
- What aspects of your business are really important to you?
- What are your hopes and dreams?
- What is your definition of success?
- What sort of turnover and income defines that success?
- How many employees does your business have?
- Why are you in business?
- What are your core values in your business?
- What impact do you want to have?
- What influence do you want to have?
- What sort of things do you want the media to be saying about you?
- What do you want your customers to be saying about you?
- How you want to be portrayed on social media?
- How many Pinterest followers do you want?
- What markets are you in? Are you local, national, or international?

Once you have completed this exercise, you will have all the material you need so that you can create the unique experience required to make your business stand out from all the others in your niche. This is the first step toward creating a brand for your business. This is the beginning of your story.

DEFINING YOUR BRAND

Whether you are responsible for defining, creating, and developing your brand in-house or you are employing a local branding and marketing agency, you will need to carry out an analysis of your business to define your brand. Completing the following exercise will help you to define and find clarity about your brand:

- A factual description of what your business is and the purpose of your business.
- Describe your product or service in one sentence.
- List all your products and/or services.
- What are the benefits and features of all of your products?
- Which are your most profitable products/services?
- Which are your most popular products/services?
- Who are your ideal customers for each of your products or services? (Consumer or business, age, gender, income, occupation, education, stage in family life cycle.)
- Out of these customers, who are the ones who are most likely to buy your most profitable products?
- Is the market and demand large enough to provide you with the number of customers you need to buy your most profitable products and achieve your financial goals?
- If your answer to the previous question is no then ask yourself the same question for each of your other products.
- Who are your three main competitors? (Have a look at their Pinterest account.)
- What distinguishes your business from your competition? What special thing are you bringing to the market that is of real value? What is your unique selling point? What solutions are your products offering your customers that will meet their needs or solve their problems?
- If you are already in business, then write down what your customers are already saying about your business. What do you think they would say about how your product or service makes them feel emotionally? (You may need to ask your customers if you do not already know.) What qualities and words would you use to describe the personality of your business as it is now? Here

are some examples of words you may wish to use: high cost, low cost, high quality, value for money, expensive, cheap, excellent customer service, friendly, professional, happy, serious, innovative, eccentric, quiet, loud, beautiful, relaxing, motivating, sincere, adventurous, amusing, charming, decisive, kind, imaginative, proactive, intuitive, loving, trustworthy, extrovert, vibrant, transparent, intelligent, creative, dynamic, resourceful.

- Now, whether you are already in business or starting out, write down all the words to describe how you want and need your brand to be perceived and what qualities you want to be associated with your brand in order to match the needs and expectations of your ideal customers. If you are already in business, hopefully this will be exactly the same from how you perceive you are at the current time.
- What is the evidence that backs up what you have said about your brand? This could be customer testimonials or any evidence about product or service quality.
- What is the biggest opportunity for your business right now?
- What products are you thinking of introducing in the near future?

HOW TO GET INTO THE MINDS AND HEARTS OF YOUR TARGET AUDIENCE

Your target audience is your most important commodity, as they are the future customers and ambassadors of your business. Every single one of them is valuable, and every single one of them can make a difference to your business. This can be because they are actually going to buy your products or simply spread the word by sharing your content on Pinterest .

However, it's a big social world out there. The possibilities of finding new people are limitless, but targeting everyone is not the solution. The biggest mistake you can make is trying to reach everyone and then not appealing to anyone. Your first step is to identify exactly who the people are who are going to be interested in your products or services, and then you need to find out everything about them. You need to get inside their heads and work out what motivates these people, what they are interested in, what their needs, hopes, aspirations, and fears are, and what are their dreams. Your product or service is the link between them and what they want. When you know this you can tailor every single message or piece of content toward them.

When you know exactly who your ideal customers are, Pinterest offers you the opportunity to go and find and reach them. It's then up to you to capture them so you can continue to communicate with them. When you know everything about your customers you are more likely to speak the right language to be able to communicate with them and build trust to the point where the next natural progression is for them to buy your product.

It's only when you truly understand your audience that you can start converting them into customers. Once you know you are targeting the right audience, you can confidently focus every ounce of your effort creating exactly the right content, nurturing them, engaging with them, and looking after them. It's only a matter of time before they will buy your product.

Creating your ideal customer persona or avatar
The following exercise is absolutely essential. Your answers to the questions will be the very information that is going to help you communicate with your customer in the right way, by providing them with the right content and the correct brand experience. Once you have done this exercise you are going to own some very powerful information. If you do not do this exercise it is very unlikely that you are going to be able to truly connect with your target audience in the way that is necessary to build trust so that you can ultimately convert them into your customers.

Your answers to the questions in the previous section will have given you a clear idea of which types of customers you need to target to give you the best chance of achieving your financial goals. You now need to find out everything about them so you can get your brand into their hearts and minds. The best way to do this is to create an imaginary persona or avatar of your ideal customer and you can build this picture by finding out the following:

- Describe your ideal customer and include the following details: are they a consumer or in business, their age, gender, income, occupation, education, and stage in family life cycle.
- Where do they live?
- What do they want most of all?
- What are their core values?
- What is their preferred lifestyle?
- What do they do on a day-to-day basis?
- What are their hopes and aspirations?
- What important truth matters to them?
- What motivates and inspires them?
- What sort of routines do they have?
- What are their day-to-day priorities?
- How do they have fun?
- What do they do in their spare time?
- What subjects are they interested in?
- Which books do they read?
- Which TV programs do they watch?
- What magazines do they read?
- Who do they follow on social media?
- Who are their role models?
- What really makes them tick?
- What are their fears and frustrations?
- What are their suspicions?
- What are their insecurities?
- What are their typical worries?

- What is the perfect solution to their worries?
- What are their dreams?
- What do they need to make them feel happy and fulfilled?

Big Questions

To answer the following questions you will need to step inside your ideal customer's mind and imagine you are them.

- How do you feel when you find your product or service? What is your initial emotional reaction?
- What are the words that go through your head?
- How can I justify buying this product for myself?
- Are you ready to buy immediately?
- Do you have any suspicions that the product may not be what it says?
- What are those suspicions? Why do you have them?
- Do you need more convincing?
- What do you need to convince you that the product is right for you?
- What do you feel when you have the product in your hand?

The reason why these are such big questions is because your answers to them will establish whether or not you have correctly defined your ideal customer and whether you have really understood their needs, desires, and fears. If you are imagining yourself as your ideal customer and you are saying "woo-hoo", ecstatically jumping up and down with glee, immediately buying the product, or relieved that you have at long last found the solution to your problem, then you have created the right avatar. If not, then you need to think again.

It's only when you have imagined yourself in the hearts and minds of your target audience that you are going to be able to connect with them on any emotional level. With the information from the above exercise, you will have everything you need to produce exactly the right content to match the needs, desires, and expectations of your ideal customer so that you can create the right brand experience and sell your products. This information is like gold.

COMMUNICATING YOUR BRAND

Once you have gone through all the processes outlined in this chapter you will have a clear idea about what your brand is, what is stands for, and how you stand out from similar businesses. You now have to work out how to best communicate this to your ideal customer so that when they hear or see your brand name they immediately make that essential emotional connection. This is what is going to make them eventually love remember your brand above all others.

When you are clear about what your brand is, what it stands for, and how you are going to stand out from other similar businesses, you then need to work out how you can communicate this message in the best possible way. Your main aim here is to create an emotional connection with your target audience that is going to help them grow to love your brand, remember your brand, and remain loyal to it. To do this you need to communicate your brand story through every aspect of your business, including your social media campaign.

With the information you now have you are armed with everything you need to create a consistent brand. If you have not already done so, you can either hand all this information over to a marketing agency or use it yourself to create all the following:

- **Your logo:** Your logo will give a clear guideline for all your promotional material, including your website or blog, stationery, templates, or any marketing material that needs to be created for online or offline promotion.
- **Your brand message: This is** the main message you want to communicate about your brand.
- **Your tagline:** A short, memorable statement about your brand

that captures the personality of your brand and communicates how you or your product will benefit your customer.

- **All your 'about' descriptions:** You can communicate your brand story through all your 'about' sections on all your social media platforms you are using.
- **The content you create for your business:** Every piece of content you create for your business needs to be tailor-made for your target audience. You will need to pick who and what subjects or topics you want to be associated with your brand, as anything you pick to write about will be a representation of your brand.
- **Your website and/or blog:** The 'about' page of your website is probably the most visited page of any website and there is a reason for this. People want to find out about your business and they want to find out what is different or special about it. This is a great place to introduce and expand on the story of your brand. This is where you can really go to town and communicate your beliefs and how you are unique. Also, the visual style of your website or blog and your unique voice should be evident throughout your site and be consistent with your brand.
- **Video content:** Videos are an incredibly powerful way of creating a personal connection with your audience. Make sure that whatever video content you produce and whatever you say is always consistent with your brand.

Chapter Eight

The Essential Pinterest Marketing Plan

BEFORE LAUNCHING INTO your campaign you will need to know exactly what you want your business to achieve and what you want to achieve through marketing your business on Pinterest. Without the necessary planning and preparation, your campaign is very unlikely to succeed.

The next few chapters take you through everything you need to do to plan your campaign before actually posting content. In this chapter you will learn how to create your mission statement, set goals and objectives, and plan the strategies and tactics you need to implement to achieve those goals. In the following chapter you will learn exactly how to prepare your business, your website and blog, and your email campaign so you can capture and convert.

Creating your Mission Statment

Many campaigns fail at the first hurdle simply because they do not have a clear idea about why they are undertaking in a campaign or what they want to achieve. They set up a Pinterest profile and have little or no idea why exactly they are doing it. "Everyone else is doing it … we probably should too." Then they launch in without first articulating the purpose of their Pinterest campaign and aimlessly start posting content. Before long, they realize that this is having no positive effect on their business, and they either give up or continue half-heartedly.

Once you have defined your brand and your target audience you will need to produce your mission statement for your social media campaign. Your mission statement is vital for your business as a whole and for your prospects and customers, and it should clearly state your commitment and promise to them as well as communicating your brand message. You will be able to include this in your Pinterest bio and on your business page. To create your mission statement, simply follow these for four easy steps:

- **Describe what your business does:** Describe exactly what you do, what you offer, and the purpose of your business.
- **Describe the way you operate:** Include your core values, your level of customer service, and your commitment to your customers. You can include how your core values contribute to the quality of your product or service.
- **Who are you doing it for?:** Who are your customers? Business owners, entrepreneurs, working women, gardeners, shop owners, etc.
- **The value you are bringing:** What benefit are you offering your customers ? What value are you bringing them?

Once you have created your statement, everyone will know exactly what you are about. You will know exactly what you need to deliver to your customers. Your employees will know what is expected of them. Your customers and prospects will know exactly what your promise is and what they can expect when buying your products and services.

Setting your Goals and Objectives

Setting goals and objectives is the key to your success on Pinterest. Once they are set you will be ready to plan and create the strategies and tactics to achieve those goals and objectives and you will be able to review and measure the success of your campaign.

Definition of a goal

A goal is a statement rooted in your business's mission and it will define what you want to accomplish and offer a broad direction for your business to follow. The three main goals of any business will ultimately be to increase sales, to reduce costs and to improve customer service and each goal will have a direct effect on the others. Here are some examples of goals and objectives within those three main goals:

1. To increase revenue and generate sales
- To increase website traffic.
- To increase brand awareness through Pinterest.
- To build a reputation as an expert within the industry.
- To build a loyal and engaged community on Pinterest.
- To increase the number of customers from word of mouth and referrals.
- To increase the number of sales.
- To increase average spend per customer.
- To increase the number of leads generated.
- To introduce new products.
- To increase online visibility.
- To promote an event.
- To build a highly targeted list of email subscribers.
- To connect with new customers.
- To build trust and build relationships with prospects and customers.
- To put a content marketing strategy in place.
- To increase business in 'X' country/state.
- To become a thought leader in your industry.
- To develop new markets by introducing product into 'X' country/state.
- To decrease spend on traditional forms of advertising and invest 'X' amount in Pinterest marketing.
- To build relationships with key influencers on Pinterest.

2. To reduce Costs
- To decrease spend on traditional forms of advertising and invest in Pinterest marketing.

3. To deliver customer satisfaction and retain customers

- To answer customer questions promptly.
- To respond to customer complaints promptly, politely and helpfully.
- To provide online help/technical support.
- To respond to customer feedback.
- To listen to your customers.

Setting measurable objectives

Once you set your broader goals then you need to get more specific and create SMART objectives (specific, measurable, attainable, relevant and time bound). Here is an explanation of exactly what each of those terms means:

- **Specific** You need to target particular areas for improvement.
- **Measurable** Your progress needs to be quantifiable and putting concrete figures on your goals is essential for success and is the only way to measure the effectiveness of your campaign.
- **Attainable / Realistic** You need to be realistic with the resources you have available and the results you are expecting need to be realistic.
- **Relevant** Your goals need to be relevant to the business climate you are in.
- **Time Bound** Make sure you set a realistic time period to achieve your goals. If a time is not set then things don't tend to get done.

Here are some examples of the sort of SMART objectives you should be setting:

- Increase sales of product X by X%
- To build an audience of X number followers on Pinterest within one year.
- To increase number of followers by X per week.
- To increase website traffic from Pinterest by X times.
- To increase opt-in list subscribers by X per week
- Increase conversions from Pinterest by X per week.
- To increase the number of leads generated from Pinterest by X per week.
- To increase the number of new customers by X per month.

- To increase the average spend per customer by X.
- Introduce X number of new products every 6 months.
- To increase sales from X country/state by X%
- To decrease spend on traditional forms of advertising by X and invest X amount in Pinterest marketing.
- To achieve a X% reach (number of people who see posts) on Pinterest.
- Utilize Pinterest to increase attendants at X event by X%.
- Utilize Pinterest to increase YouTube views by X people per week.

Choosing your Strategies and Tactics

Once you have set your quantifiable goals and objectives you are going to have to work out how you are going to accomplish them using Pinterest. You will need to think about the strategies and tactics you are going to use and they need to be quantifiable as well. Here are some examples of the strategies you may want to implement:

- To follow 'X' number of users per week.
- To post content on Pinterest 'X' number of times per day.
- To create 'X' number of blog posts per week/month and post and images on Pinterest to promote them.
- To post 'X' offers per month/6 months on Pinterest.
- To run 'X' number of competitions/contests per year on Pinterest.
- To create 'X' videos on YouTube per month and post of Pinterest.
- To spend 'X' minutes per day following new users.
- To spend 'X' minutes per day liking, commenting and sharing followers pins.
- To follow 'X' number of influencers on Pinterest per week.
- Contribute to 'X' number of collaborative boards.
- Comment on 'X' number of relevant pins on the popular section per week.
- Select a 'Pinner per month'

- Try and win at least one 'Pinner of the month' competition per year.

Of course at the beginning you are going to need to make an educated guess at the number of times you are going to need to do one thing to achieve another. As your campaign runs you will need to adjust certain aspects to achieve what you set out to achieve. For example, you may need to create more pins to increase the number of visits to your website or you may need to follow more accounts to increase your number of followers.

The only way you can do this is by constantly monitoring and measuring your results against the original goals and objectives you set and adjusting your campaign accordingly.

Creating your Pinterest Posting Calendar

Now that you have your strategies in place, you will have a good idea of the amount and type of content you need to post to achieve those objectives. One of the most challenging tasks of your Pinterest campaign is going to be to consistently deliver a high standard of content to your fans on a daily basis. You are going to need to post between one to four times a day. This does not mean you need to create numerous blog articles each day, but you are going to need to communicate in some way and find unique ways for your audience to interact with your brand and offer some kind of value on a regular basis. This may seem daunting to begin with, but you will be surprised just how one idea leads to another.

To help you map out your content for the next six months or the year ahead, you need to create a Pinterest posting calendar which is going to be your key to consistent posting. There are many online tools and apps that can help you with this. Google Calendar is a very good calendar to use, and it lets you color code the different types of posts. You can also use Hootsuite, the social media dashboard, to plot out your calendar or use a spreadsheet in Excel. There are also other online applications, like www.trello.com, which has easy to use drag-and-drop features. Using mind-mapping applications like 'Simplemind' can really help when brainstorming for content ideas.

To get started you will simply need to map out and schedule the days of the week for each week of the year and decide what types of post you are going to create for certain days. You will need to balance the type of content in order to create variety and interest for your audience. You then need to create topics or themes and then break the year down into weeks/months and make a schedule. You can then add all the things that you are planning within your business, like offers, contests, product launches, and webinars, and then add all the things going on outside your business, like public holidays and special events. You then need to incorporate all that information into your daily action plan.

It may seem daunting to look at a blank calendar, but you will be surprised how it comes together when you start breaking it down into months, weeks, and days. A posting calendar will help you keep your campaign focused, on track, and in line with your brand and your marketing goals and also keep it balanced in terms of the subject and type of media you use. A calendar will help you look ahead and help you to incorporate your marketing plan into your Pinterest campaign. It may be that you are launching a new product, or maybe certain products tie in with specific holidays. You may have certain industry events you need to attend or are perhaps creating your own. Maybe you are going to run a competition at a certain time of the year. Whatever it is you are planning throughout the year, you need to include it on your calendar.

Chapter Nine

Preparing your Business for Success

WHETHER YOUR SITE is being found through an organic search, an advertising campaign, Pinterest, or any other social media platform, all your hard work is going to be wasted unless you have put a system in place to capture leads and convert them into customers. This system has to start from the moment your prospect either hits your website, your blog, or your Pinterest profile, and your ultimate goal is to convert your browsers into buyers.

Firstly, the unfortunate fact is that the majority of your website visitors are unlikely to buy from you on their first visit. If you do not have a website that grabs their attention within the first couple of seconds, then they will move very quickly onto another site. Secondly, even if your site does catch their eye, they are still likely to check out other sites and still may not return. To make any kind of impact at all your site needs to grab their attention and then capture their email address so you can continue your relationship with them through email. This chapter is going to take you through steps you will need to take, from getting your website or blog ready to setting up and creating your email campaign.

Email is still one of the most powerful ways to convert prospects into customers and has a conversion rate three times higher than social media conversion rates. That is not to say that your Pinterest campaign is any less important, as this is where you are going to find and nurture your leads and transfer them to your opt-in by either capturing them on Pinterest or on your website or blog. This chapter is going to take you through steps you will need to take from getting your website or blog ready to setting up and creating your email campaign.

Preparing your Website for Success

Whether you already have a website or blog or you are creating a new site from scratch, you need to make sure it has the necessary features to grab the attention of your target audience and capture their email addresses. Capturing the email addresses of your target audience has to be one of your most important goals when creating your website. Once your prospects have voluntarily submitted their email address, you have the opportunity to build a relationship, communicate your message, and promote your products and services on an ongoing and regular basis. A well thought-out and crafted email campaign can immediately establish trust and favor with your subscribers. Don't forget that it is you who owns your opt-in list and nobody can take it away from you. As long as you are providing your subscribers value with great content, they are likely to want to keep hearing from you. Remember you cannot rely on social media to continue your relationship as these platforms are changing all the time. You need to build your email list.

Once you have completed the exercise in the branding section and have your ideal customer persona or avatar, you will have a clear picture of what your target audience's pain point or problem is and how your product can help solve their problem or make their life better in some way. If you have a blog, and most businesses today need a blog, you will also have all the tools you need to create the right content to attract your target audience. Armed with this information you are halfway ready to putting a system in place to sell, so your products sell themselves and your website is working like an extra sales person selling your products 24/7.

When your visitor arrives at your site, you have only three seconds to grab their attention. You need to connect emotionally with them and let them know immediately that they have arrived at the right place by communicating exactly how you are going to help them and what it is you are offering them.

Once they are on your site, you then need to win their interest and confidence so that they will voluntarily submit their email address. To do this you will need to create a lead magnet and offer your audience something which is incredibly valuable to them for free. There are numerous ways you can do this and which one you use will depend very much on what type of business you are and what your goals are. If you are a business offering technical solutions, then you could offer them a free trial. If you are offering information, then you could offer them a free report, a short video training series, or an ebook. If you are selling some kind of product or service, you could offer them a money-off voucher. These work particularly well for restaurants and the service industry as a whole. Whatever you are offering, it needs to be really good to attract your audience and get them to volunteer their email.

Here are the features you need to have on your website or blog or any landing page with a special offer.

- **Keep your design simple:** Your site needs to have a clean and simple design, and you need to communicate your most important message clearly and concisely to your target audience. Your most important content with any call-to-action needs to be placed above the fold, where they will be easily seen, and your call-to-action should have an easily seen button link rather than just a text link.
- **Make your site easy to navigate:** Really this is so important. Try to use the minimum number of pages you can and make your menu titles as easy to understand as possible.
- **Clearly communicate your message:** You want your visitors to subscribe to your opt-in, so you need to place your compelling offer with an image and title of the offer somewhere where it is visible. The message and benefit of your offer needs be descriptive and specific.

- **Add a clear call-to-action:** In order for your visitors to sign up, they will need to be told what to do. Make sure you have a direct call-to-action, for example, "Download your free ebook now" or "Sign up for your discount voucher now." Your call-to-action needs to be clearly visible with an eye-catching button link which is much more effective than a text link.

- **Add clear contact information:** Make it easy for your prospects to contact you by placing your contact details where they will be easily seen. With the technology available, you can even add chat features so that as soon as your prospect arrives on your site a chat form appears asking if you can be of any assistance. Obviously you need the resources to be able to man this, but it is an incredibly powerful way of quickly building trust and showing how much you value your website visitors by being available to answer any of their questions.

- **Email capture form:** Your email capture form needs to be as simple as possible, preferably just asking for their name and email. You need to state on the form that their email address is safe with you and will not be shared with anyone. Make sure your form is in a prominent position and consider using a pop-up form that appears after 20 seconds after your prospect has arrived on your site. Your email sign-up form needs to go at the top, side, and bottom of your webpage and also on your 'about page,' which is often the most popular page on your site.

- **Privacy policy:** You need a clear privacy policy on your website and to make it clear that you will not be spamming them or selling their information.

- **Thank you page:** Once your visitor has completed the form, you will have them as a lead, but before you let them go you can send them to a thank you page where you can offer them the opportunity to share your offer with their friends by including social sharing buttons.

- **Mobile Friendly:** You need to make sure your offer is easily visible and easy to complete on a mobile phone. This is incredibly

important, as more and more people are purchasing from their mobiles. There is nothing more annoying for the user than if the site is hard to navigate from their mobile.
- Don't add external links to other sites. Be careful not to fall into the trap of wanting to make your site more interesting by adding lots of content and links to other external sites, as this will only detract from your main goals and you'll end up sending traffic away from your site.

Landing pages

Landing pages are incredibly effective if you want to promote specific offers for specific products to specific audiences. A landing page is a page that is designed to give information about an offer and then capture a lead with a form for your visitor to complete so that the visitor can download or claim that offer. Landing pages are highly effective in capturing leads because they are designed to be specific in their goal, which is to capture the contact information of your visitor.

The landing page should have a clear, uncluttered design and not have any links or navigation menus that could take your visitor away from the landing page. It should contain the following:

- A headline (The title of the offer)
- A description of the offer, clearly detailing the benefits to your visitor
- A compelling image of the offer
- A clear call-to-action. This can be in the form of an image or text.
- A form to capture contact information (The fewer fields that are required to be completed, the more leads you will receive.)
- A clear privacy policy on your website that makes it clear that you will not be spamming them or selling their information
- A thank you page leading them to another offer or social sharing

You can either ask your web developer to create landing pages or there are numerous tools available on the Internet where you can easily create one, for example: www.leadpages.net, www.unbounce.com, www.launcheffect.com, and www.instapage.com

SETTING UP AND CREATING YOUR EMAIL CAMPAIGN

Once you have created your lead capture system on your website, blog, or separate landing page and have your subscribers' permission to send them your email, you are going to need a really good email campaign to convert those leads into sales.

Email is still one of the most effective forms of converting leads into sales, and email is more powerful than ever. Not only is it cost effective but it also provides one of the most direct and personal lines of communication with your customer. Once subscribed, they have invited you into their inbox on a regular basis and producing valuable content for your subscribers will develop trust and deepen your relationship with your subscribers. Your email will also work hand in hand with your Pinterest campaign. As you build your relationship with your followers on Pinterest, they are more likely to deem your emails valuable and open them.

The first thing you need to do is set yourself up with a good email marketing provider and there are many you can choose from: www.aweber.com, www.constantcontact.com, and www.mailchimp.com to name a few. It's important to use a system where you have a confirmed opt-in. This is when the subscriber is sent an email to confirm their email address. This confirms that you are gaining consent and legally protects you. It also helps you to keep a clean list, and it protects you from sending emails to incorrect addresses. You can then automate your emails with an auto responder and send out emails automatically over time.

Your next task is to plan and create your email campaign. Here are a few tips for doing so:

- **Be clear about your goals:** You need to be absolutely clear from day one what you want to achieve through email. Are you using it to introduce a new product at some time? Are you launching an event? Whatever you do, make sure you know exactly what it is that you want to achieve.
- **Keep it simple and in line with your branding:** Make sure your email design ties in with your branding. Most email providers offer templates which you can add your own branding to, or you can get a designer to create a particular design. Keep it really simple. Sometimes if things are too fancy they become impersonal.
- **Send a regular newsletter:** Plan to send a regular newsletter email at least once a month and once a week if you can. You can also plan to send off information about offers which tie in with special holidays and occasions throughout the year or competitions or events that you may be planning.
- **Plan your topics:** You need to plan the topics you want to cover in each email, and this should tie in nicely with the plan for your blog articles. You then need to deliver high quality content which is tailor-made to fit with your subscribers' interests, and it needs to be so good that they are looking forward to the next email from you. If you are sending emails about offers then you need to show them clearly how these offers are going to benefit their lives.
- **Attention-grabbing titles:** This is where you need to get really creative. Your main goal here is to get your subscriber to open your email, and you need to create a headline that is going to make your subscriber curious and inquisitive and eager to open your mail. Questions work really well as titles, and you will often see your open rates increase. This is because people find questions intriguing and they feel like you are directly addressing them. Try and avoid the words that will trigger spam filters. Simply search Google for a list of these words to avoid.

- **Be authentic and true to your brand:** Write your emails in a style that your audience will grow to recognize, 'like,' and identify with your brand. Write so your subscriber feels like you are just writing to them. You need to establish yourself as a likeable expert for your subscribers. Try and create a personal relationship with them by addressing them by name and giving them a warm friendly introduction. Offering them the opportunity to connect with you and answer any of their questions by simply replying to your mail is a great way to create a connection and trust.
- **Keep it simple** Make sure your emails are simply constructed and straight to the point so you keep your subscribers' interest and get them quickly to the place you want them to go, like your blog or offer.
- **Include social sharing buttons:** Include all your social sharing icons and links in your mail.
- **Make them feel safe:** Make sure your subscribers are clear that their email will not be shared and that they can unsubscribe anytime.
- **Analyze your open rates:** Most email service providers include statistics in their packages so you can analyze open rates, bounce rates, click through rates, unsubscribers, and social sharing statistics. These results give you the opportunity to find out what is and what is not working.

Chapter Ten

Blog Blog Blog

THIS CHAPTER IS for anyone who does not have a blog. The word blog has been mentioned numerous times throughout the book and has become an essential part of any online business today.

What is a Blog?

A blog (short for web log) is a term used to describe a website that provides an ongoing journal of individual news stories which are based around a certain subject or subjects (blog posts). Blogs have given people the power of the media. Anyone can now create a personal type of news that appeals to a high number of small niche audiences.

Bloggers simply complete a simple online form with a title and body and then post it. The blog post then appears at the top of the website as the most recent article. Over time, the posts build up to become a collection, which are then archived chronologically for easy reference. Each blog post can be a discussion with space for comments below the post where readers can leave comments and questions. This is where bloggers start to build relationships and a community with their readers and other bloggers who may have similar interests. Blogs were one of the earliest forms of social media, and they started growing in the late 1990s. The number of blogs has exploded in recent years, and they now underpin the majority of successful social media campaigns.

Why Blog for Business?

Blogging is one of the most beneficial tools that a business has to communicate its expertise and ideas to its prospects and customers and to engage with them. Businesses can share information about their business and about any subject that may be of interest to their niche. It is a fact that businesses with blogs benefit from an increase in the number of visitors to their website, increased leads, an increase in inbound links, and increased sales. Here are some of the reasons why and the benefits that come with blogging:

- **Underpins your whole social media campaign:** Your blog is the focus of all your social media efforts and the center of all your content marketing efforts. One of the main goals of any business today will be to get people to their blog to read their valuable and targeted content. Social media will be one of the main tools they can use to drive traffic to their blog.
- **Increased website traffic:** A well-optimized blog will increase your chances of being found in searches. Google loves unique, fresh content, and if this is created regularly, it will boost your traffic.
- **Builds brand awareness**: A blog offers a business the opportunity to build a community and awareness for their products or services. The more people who see your blog, the more people see your brand.
- **Provides valuable information for your niche:** Creating a blog gives your business a voice and provides your niche with valuable information in relation to the subjects they are interested in. This may include information about market trends, industry news, and insight into your products and services and what is behind them.
- **Thought leadership:** Sharing your expertise with valuable information will make you stand out as a thought leader in your particular field and help you build a professional online reputation.
- **Builds trust & creates warm leads:** When you are providing valuable content for your niche on a regular basis, answering their questions, and addressing their concerns, this in turn creates trust between you and your prospective customers. This trust leads to more leads and will result in sales. When your audience becomes regular readers of your blog, they become warm rather than cold leads. The ice has been broken, and they

are halfway there in terms of buying your product.

- **You gain more knowledge:** While writing your blog you will be continually researching your subject, learning about new technology, products, and trends. In turn, this keeps you ahead of the game. In the eyes of your customers, it makes you an expert. As time goes by you become more and more knowledgable and can steer your business in line with market trends and keep your products and services up to the minute. You will also find that blogging is inspiring and your ideas will snowball. As you learn more, you will find more material to blog about.
- **Interaction and feedback:** When your blog has room for comments and discussion it will give you the opportunity to hear what people are saying, the questions they are asking, and insight into what they want out of your products. Feedback like this is invaluable to your business, and it also leads to more ideas for more blog posts. This kind of feedback also encourages a conversation, and you actually get the opportunity to communicate with prospective customers.

How to Create a Blog

Creating your blog is incredibly straightforward. There are a number of free blogging platforms that are available. However, if you read the terms and conditions of most of these platforms you will find that at the end of the day you do not actually own the content and you will not have full control of your blog. You will have no control of the advertising displayed, you are unlikely to be able to include an email capture form, you will not be able to have you own domain name, and you will not be able to install plugins. With a free platform, your domain name will look something like http://mybusinessblog.theirblogplatformname.com. Overall, it is not going to look that professional.

The best and safest way of creating a blog and running with your own domain name is to create one with wordpress.org or you can use website creators like www.wix.com or www.squarespace.com. Both website creators offer blogs with their product, and you can add your own domain. Using any of these will give you full control over your site.

Wordpress.org is a free open source platform, which means it can be modified and customized by anyone. You can use custom themes or choose from hundreds of free themes and plugins. The wordpress.org blogging platform is free, but you will need to purchase a domain name and host your site on your own server. However, most hosting companies offer inexpensive monthly plans and a one-click installation solution. You will also need to make sure you backup your blog. You may very well find that this is included in your hosting package.

WHAT MAKES A SUCCESSFUL BLOG?

Creating your blog is incredibly straightforward. There are a number of free blogging platforms that are available. However, if you read the terms and conditions of most of these platforms you will find that at the end of the day you do not actually own the content and you will not have full control of your blog. You will have no control of the advertising displayed, you are unlikely to be able to include an email capture form, you will not be able to have you own domain name, and you will not be able to install plugins. With a free platform, your domain name will look something like http://mybusinessblog.theirblogplatformname.com. Overall, it is not going to look that professional.

The best and safest way of creating a blog and running with your own domain name is to create one with wordpress.org or you can use website creators like www.wix.com or www.squarespace.com. Both website creators offer blogs with their product, and you can add your own domain. Using any of these will give you full control over your site.

Wordpress.org is a free open source platform, which means it can be modified and customized by anyone. You can use custom themes or choose from hundreds of free themes and plugins. The wordpress.org blogging platform is free, but you will need to purchase a domain name and host your site on your own server.

However, most hosting companies offer inexpensive monthly plans and a one-click installation solution. You will also need to make sure you backup your blog. You may very well find that this is included in your hosting package.

11 Things a Blog should have

An incentive to join your opt-in
One of the main goals of your blog is to captures leads. The majority of your readers will probably only read one of your blog posts so it's really important to try and get them on your opt-in list so they will keep reading your blog. You will need to make sure you give them some kind of incentive to complete the email capture form, like a free report, free ebook, or simply email updates.

An engaging image
A blog needs at least one image to make it look interesting and inviting. Blogs without images are simply boring. You can use your own images, stock photos, or images from photo sharing sites like Flickr.

Clear call-to-actions
You need to make it very clear both within your text and outside your text what you want your readers to do. This could be anything from signing up for email updates, a free trial, a free offer, a request for a quote, or more information on a product.

Email capture form
You can either include a prominent form on your blog or install a pop-up mail capture form. If you do install a pop-up then make sure the reader has a good few seconds to read the heading and start reading the article before the form pops up. It is also a good practice to put at least three email sign-up forms on the page, one below the article, one in the footer, and one on the top beside the article or right above it.

About section

Your "about" section is the introduction to you and your blog. It's probably the most viewed page of any blog. People like to know who is writing the blog and feel acquainted with that person, so you need to get your personality over in this section. Make sure you include your name and a picture of yourself. This will help your readers make a personal connection with you. A video of yourself is also a great a way of getting your readers acquainted too. Above all, focus on how you are going to help your readers, what problems you are going to solve for them, and introduce some of the topics you are going to talk about. Remember, your blog is about your audience's needs and not yours.

Contact page

A simple contact form works best but also make it really easy for people to reach out to you. Make sure you include all your social sharing buttons and an email capture form.

Easy to search archives

If the content of your blog posts is interesting, then your readers are going to want to read more so you need to make the previous blog posts easily accessible. On many sites it really is incredibly difficult to find content, so you will need to get yourself a custom archive page. A search box at the top of your blog is a great idea for helping your readers find content.

Social sharing plug-ins

You need to include buttons or links to all the social networks where you have a presence. There are hundreds of plug-ins you can use to do this. Also make sure you have sharing buttons next to your articles as well.

RSS Feed

RSS (Rich Site Summary) is a format for delivering regularly changing content on the Internet. It saves you from checking the sites you are interested in for new content. Instead, it retrieves the content from sites you are interested in. Make sure you have the RSS feed and then have a clear call-to-action making it clear why they should subscribe to your feed. If you want to keep up-to-date with your favorite bloggers you can sign up to either My Yahoo, www.bloglines.com, or www.newsgator.com.

Comments section

Your blog needs a comment section which will encourage interaction and help you to build relationships with your readers. You can install Facebook comments easily with a WordPress plug-in. Disqus is another favorite comment provider.

A guest bloggers welcome page

Guest posting is becoming more and more important in the blogging community and making it obvious that you will accept guest posts is going to go a long way to building relationships with other bloggers. The benefits of having other people contributing to your blog are that you will have more valuable content on your site and more exposure if your guest blogger promotes their posts on their site. You may also gain from the opportunity to produce a guest post on their blog at a later date. Guest blogging is a top method of getting back links to your blog, which is essential for search engine optimization.

Privacy policy & terms of service pages
Make it clear your email readers are safe with you and you are not going to share their information with any other parties.

PROMOTING YOUR BLOG

If you want to run a successful blog, you cannot just rely on search to get it out into the blogosphere. You need to find other ways of promoting your content and getting found.

- **Promote on your social sites:** Posting your blog content on social sites is essential. You can connect your blog to Twitter and Facebook so your content is automatically shared. Or you can use Hootsuite or Tweetdec to share your content to multiple sites, which will save you time. When posting, use an image to grab your audience's attention and make sure you use popular hashtags for your topic which will open up more opportunities to being found by new people.
- **Guest blogging:** Guest blogging is a great way of gaining a larger following. It will also give your blog more exposure, credibility, and increase your inbound links, which is essential for SEO. Most bloggers allow guest bloggers to post their bio, including their social profiles and blog URL, on their site.
- **Social sharing buttons:** As mentioned previously, it is essential to have social sharing buttons next to your blog articles.
- **Comment on other blogs:** There is so much opportunity for you to promote yourself today with the number of blogs and social sites. If you comment on other peoples' blogs you can often leave a URL, but only if it is relevant to the article being

commented on and you are adding some value to the article.
- **Website and email:** If you have a website then try and point people to your blog. You can do this by adding visual links on your "about" page and other pages. Also make sure you have a link to your blog in your email and send an email to your current contacts telling them about your blog.
- **Create a Google Adwords campaign:** If you are serious about driving traffic to your site and generating leads and you have your blog set up to catch leads and subscribers, an Adwords campaign may kick start your traffic while you are waiting for your blog to get found naturally in search results. Getting quick results like this will also allow you to see if your blog design and format is working and whether any incentives you are offering are enough to generate subscribers and leads.
- **Submit your blog to Reddit and Stumbleupon:** Both of these websites allow their uses to rate web content. Reddit is a collection of webpages which have been submitted by its users. Stumbleupon is a collection of web pages that has been given the thumbs up. You can submit pages directly on its submit page or by installing the Firefox add-on or the Chrome extension. It is best not add too many of your own pages to Stumbleupon but make sure you add both the Reddit and Stumbleupon buttons to your blog so other people can.

THE ESSENTIAL WORDPRESS PLUGINS

One of the best things about WordPress for your blog is that it is easy to customize and you need little or no technical or design knowledge to create a great blog. There are a ton of plug-ins you can install to make your site even better, but there are so many it is difficult to choose which ones are really important. To help you, here are some plug-ins that are essential for your blog:

- **The Facebook comments plugin:** Installing Facebook comments into your blog can be tricky, but with this easy to use plugin you can easily administer and customize Facebook comments from your WordPress site. Another plugin, **Facebook comments SEO,** will insert a Facebook comment form, Open Graph tags, and insert all Facebook comments into your WordPress database for better search engine optimization. When it comes to spammers, Facebook with Open Graph is managing to weed out spammers and trolls with great effectiveness. Facebook allows you to login with Facebook, Yahoo, and Microsoft Live.

- **Disqus comment system:** The other popular comment system Disqus replaces your WordPress comment system with comments hosted and powered by Disqus. It features threaded comments and replies, notifications and replies by email, aggregated comments and social mentions, full spam filtering, and black-and-white lists. Disqus allows you to login with Facebook, Twitter, and Google.
- **Facebook Chat:** This is great if you want to chat with your visitors in real time. When installed, Facebook Chat will display on the bottom right. This is great for supplying support on your site.
- **Broken Link Checker:** This essential plugin scans your site and notifies you if it finds any broken links or missing images and then lets you replace the link with one that works.
- **RB Internal Links:** This plugin assists you with internal links and cuts the risk of error pages and broken links.
- **Social Sharing Plugins:** There are numerous social sharing plugins available for WordPress. **Flare** is a simple yet eye-catching sharing bar that you can customize depending on which buttons you want to display. It helps to get you followed or 'liked' and helps get your content shared via posts, pages, and media types. The other great feature Flare has is that you can display your Flare at the top, bottom, or right of your post content. When Flare is displayed on the left and right of your posts, it follows your visitors down the page and conveniently hides when

not needed. Other social sharing plugins include: **Floating Social Media Icon, Social Stickers,** and **Shareaholic,** to name but a few.

- **All-In-One Schema Rich Snippets:** Rich snippets are markup tags that webmasters can put in their sites in order to tell Google what type of content they have on their site so that Google can better display it in search results. It is basically a short summary of your page. Rich snippets are very interactive, let you stand out from your competition, and help with your search engine ranking. Unless you are a techie then implementing them can be tricky. However, this plugin makes it really simple by giving you a meta box to fill in every time you create a new blog post.
- **Contact Form Plugins:** It is very important to make it easy for your visitors to contact you, and a form really does help with this. There are numerous plugins available for you to easily install, and here are a few: **Contact 7, Fast Secure Contact form, Contact form, and Contactme.**
- **Simple Pull Quote:** The Simple Pull Quote WordPpress plugin provides an easy way for you to insert and pull quotes into your blog posts. This is great for bringing attention to important pieces of information and adding interest to a post.
- **Backup Plugins:** Backing up your files and database is essential. It may be that your hosting service provides this, but there are very good plugins that do this: Vaultpress, BackWPup, Backup buddy, and Backup.
- **Related Posts Plugins:** Related post plugins help your visitors to stay on your site by analyzing the content on your site and pulling in similar articles from your site for them to read. One of the most popular ones is **nrelate related** content which is simple to install and activate. **WordPress related posts** is another one.
- **Search Everything Plugin:** This plugin increases the ability of the WordPress search, and you can configure it to search for anything you choose.
- **Google Analytics Plugin:** The Google Analytics plugin allows

you to easily integrate Google Analytics using Google Analytics tracking code.
- **Google XML Sitemaps:** It is essential that the search engines can index your site and this plugin will generate a special XML sitemap.
- **SEO Friendly images:** This plugin automatically adds alt and title attributes to all your images, which helps to improve traffic from search engines.
- **Akismet (Comments and Spam):** The more traffic you receive, the more likely it is for you to receive spam and fake comments. Akismet checks your comments against Akismet web services to see if they look like spam or not and then lets you review it under your comments admin screen.
- **Social Author Bio:** Social Author Bio automatically adds an author box along with Gravatar and social icons on posts.
- **Thank Me Later:** This great little plugin automatically sends a thank you note by email to anyone who has commented on your blog. You can personalize your email and set up exactly when you want to send it, and you can set it up to only send it out once or as a chain of emails. This plugin is great for engaging people who comment on your blog, and you could use it to encourage people to join your opt-in.

MEASURING YOUR RESULTS

Measuring the success of your blog is crucial in order to steer your blog in the right direction so that your business can benefit from all the rewards a top blog can offer. Here are a number of ways you can measure your success:

Google Analytics

You can easily measure the number of social media shares, number of leads, subscribers, and comments on your blog. For more detailed information on your blog performance, setting up a Google Analytics account is essential and will offer you a wealth of detailed information so you can measure results, including the following:

- **The number of back links:** In the left side bar under **Standard Reports** you will find a section **Traffic Sources,** and then under **Social,** you will find **Trackbacks**. You will find here any web pages that have linked to any page of your site with the number of visits.
- **The number of visits:** Obviously this is one of the most important statistics, and you will be able to see easily how many visits you have and information about where your traffic is coming from.
- **Page views:** You will be able to see which pages are generating the most interest, and therefore, you will be able to plan more content similar to this.
- **Keywords:** You can keep track of your success with how your traffic is being generated by keywords. You will be able to see if your optimization for certain keywords are working and whether your blog is being found by keywords that you had not considered. When you identify which keywords are the most popular, you can try and work them into other blog posts.
- **Conversions:** In Google Analytics you will also be able to track conversions, which is an action on your site that is important to your business. This could be a download, sign up, or purchase. You will need to define your goals in analytics in order to track the conversion. You will be able to see conversion rates and also the value of conversions if you set a monetary value. There are detailed instructions available in Google Analytics on how to set this up, or you can employ a web developer or specialist to set this up.

Chapter Eleven

The Icing on the Cake!

FOLLOWING ALL THE steps, instructions, and strategies is going to go a long way to making your campaign succeed, but what does it take to make you really good? If you have ever followed or are following certain brands on social media, you will probably have discovered that there are certain brands or businesses that stand out from the crowd. These are the brands and businesses that seem bigger than their products. These are the ones who usually have a sizeable and highly targeted audience, the best quality content, the greatest amount of interaction and engagement, and often post viral content. They literally have their audience hanging on their every word and get the highest open rates for their emails. They appear to understand their audience and relate to them by going out of their way by either helping them to achieve their dreams, calm their fears or confirm their suspicions, and offer them incredible value. It is obvious by the interaction that they have built a loving and respecting community, and you can be almost sure that all this is transferring to their balance sheets. These businesses are what I call 'The Social Media Superstars.' They are the game changers and they truly know how to leverage the power of social media to work for their business.

These 'Social Media Superstars' can often be compared to those party animals, the ones who always seem to be the most popular at any party and are more often than not surrounded by an audience of engaged and happy people having a great time. These people also always seem to be the most interesting, the most interested, the most charismatic, and the most engaged. They almost always tend to be good listeners as well. So how can you emulate this scenario, and what does it take to stand out from the crowd in Pinterest marketing?

It's all about your audience and a few other things!
The reasons these individuals, businesses, and brands are good at social media marketing is not because they have particular powers. It's not by chance or coincidence. It's because they know that it's all about the audience and a few other things!

Of course your aim is to ultimately benefit your business, but in order to do this you need to make it all about your audience and what they want. If you give them what they want by either making their life better or easier in some way or solving a problem they may have, then you are going to build a valuable base of fans who trust you, open your emails, and are ready to go to the next step and buy your product. You will find that your fans will become ambassadors and advocates and will then be doing the work for you by sharing your content and promoting your brand in the most powerful way, word-of-mouth. To achieve this and stand out from the crowd, you need to go the extra mile by doing the following:

- Being fully committed and positive about your campaign and in it for the long term
- Totally believing in what you are offering. This could be your product, your service, or yourself, if you are a personal brand.
- Making it all about your audience, knowing exactly who they are, what makes them tick, what they need, and how to connect with them
- Putting your audience's needs above your own and demonstrating the rich content and service you provide
- Putting the relationship with your audience first, by listening to them, understanding them, and embracing conversation where you can
- Offering your audience incredible value with free information and advice
- Being authentic and true to your brand

So if there is one piece of insight I want to leave you with, it is this:

IT'S ALL ABOUT YOUR AUDIENCE and WHAT THEY WANT

I really hope you have enjoyed the book, that you have found it of great value, and that you will continue using it as your manual for your success on Pinterest. The world of social media is continually changing, and it is my commitment to keep updating the books as and when these changes happen. If you would like to continue receiving these social media updates by email, please sign up at www.alexstearn.com

I would love your feedback about the book and would be very grateful if you could take just a moment to leave a review on Amazon at this link . By leaving a review, you can also enter the Prize draw for a Kindle Fire HD at this link and, of course, please feel free to contact me if you have any questions, at alex@alexstearn.com

I have also written a series covering all the major social media platforms, including:Facebook Twitter, Google + , Pinterest, Instagram, Tumblr, YouTube. If you are planning be purchase more I would suggest that purchasing the big book would be better value, Make Social Media Work for your Business is available on Amazon from $9.99

Lastly, I have also set up a group on Facebook called 'Make Social Media Work for your Business.' The group was created for supporting each other in our social media efforts, for networking, and also as a place for finding out about the latest social media developments. You can join at this link: Join Now

I will also be continually posting helpful and inspirational tips on my Pinterest, and I look forward to connecting with you there or on any of your preferred social networks

Make Pinterest Work For Your Business

Website: www.alexstearn.com
www.pinterest.com/alexstearn
www.facebook.com/alexandrastearn
www.instagram.com/alexstearn
www.twitter.com/alexstearncom
www.alexstearn.tumblr.com
www.youtube.com/alexstearn
www.linkedin.com/in/alexstearn
www.google.com/+alexstearn

Other Books in the Series

Make Social Media Work For Your Business
The complete series in one book!
The complete guide to marketing your business, generating new leads, finding new customers and building your brand on Twitter, LinkedIn, Tumblr, Pinterest, Instagram, YouTube, Google, +Facebook, Foursquare, Vine and Snapchat.

Make Facebook Work for your Business

Make Instagram Work for your Business

Make Twitter Work for your Business

Make Google + Work for your Business

Make YouTube Work for your Business

Make Tumblr Work for your Business

Win a Kindle Fire HD

To enter the prize draw simply write a review for this book on Amazon.com and then complete the entry at [this link] Good Luck!

www.ingramcontent.com/pod-product-compliance
Lightning Source LLC
Chambersburg PA
CBHW051716170526
45167CB00002B/676